GREECE

Recipes by **EMILY LYCOPOLUS**
Photos by **DL ACKEN**

GREECE

RECIPES
FOR OLIVE OIL AND
VINEGAR LOVERS

TOUCHWOOD EDITIONS

CONTENTS

INTRODUCTION

The thing I possibly love most about Greek cooking is that it tends to use spices in places that I wouldn't necessarily expect in a particular dish or paired with a specific food. In fact, some of the spice selections in Greek recipes are positively eyebrow-raising for people who are encountering Greek food for the first time. And yet, the flavors inevitably meld and create the most complex, refreshing tastes. Think of the combination of cinnamon and allspice in tomato sauce, for example. How unexpected! But it is undeniably delicious.

Many of the recipes in this book have gradually become everyday staples in my household, mainly because I've taken traditional recipes and tweaked and refined them to the point where they're incorporated into my daily routine. I now rarely buy Greek yogurt, for example, as it's so easy to make, and there's something so satisfying about getting up in the morning to a lovely fresh pot of it. And it's so versatile! Spoon some cherries on top for breakfast, whisk it into a salad dressing for lunch, or use it to whip up a quick batch of tzatziki, savoring each mouthful even more because you know you've made every part of it.

Of course, no cuisine is without its quirks, and it can be quite a challenge to keep a selection of fresh herbs and spices on hand at all times just in case you have a hankering for Greek food. That's where fused and infused olives oils and balsamic vinegars come in. In this book, I've chosen to feature two of each that I use all the time when I cook Greek recipes (plus, of course, the ever-reliable, ever-versatile extra virgin olive oil!). The oils and vinegars used within these pages simplify the process of creating complex and delicious recipes out of basic, everyday ingredients. Note that apricots have a very limited season in North America and some traditional Greek ingredients will require a trip to a specialty store. If you happen to have the following olive oils and vinegars in your pantry, however, you're set.

These two oils and two vinegars will transform everyday Greek favorites into dishes that your family and friends just can't get enough of.

I do hope that you'll enjoy these recipes as much as we do, that they spur fun and interesting conversation and ensure everyone lingers at the table a little longer.

Fused or infused?

In the olive oil world, the term "fused" is used to refer to olive oil made with the agrumato method; fresh citrus fruit is added to the whole olives, and they are crushed together to extract oil. "Infused" is the term used when herbs or spices are pressed separately and then paired with the olive oil. Both methods ensure the best flavor and standards of food safety. Note that fusing or infusing olive oil should never be done at home. Do your research and always purchase fresh extra virgin olive oil from a reputable source.

LEMON
FUSED
OLIVE OIL

Created by the agrumato method of crushing fresh olives and lemons together, this oil is bright, subtle, and all things lemon. I use it in baking, for frying, and for grilling. It goes in almost everything and is always the bottle that is finished first in my cupboard, no matter how often I refill it.

Lemon fused olive oil adds a lovely brightness that isn't quite as intense as that of fresh lemon juice. Sometimes when I really want a punch of lemon, I'll use them together, but more often, the creamy soft lemon imparted from this olive oil is perfect by itself.

GARLIC INFUSED OLIVE OIL

One of the challenges I find with Greek food is that, because the flavors of mint, parsley, oregano, dill, and even fennel are quite subtle, when you use fresh garlic, it tends to overpower everything else in the dish, especially when it comes to leftovers. But there is a solution! Using Garlic infused olive oil prevents that from happening and ensures that leftovers on Day Three taste just as delicious as they did straight from the oven. Better known as my "lazy oil," this is beyond a pantry staple. Whenever I don't want to deal with peeling, crushing, or mincing garlic, I turn to this liquid miracle! Drizzling this oil is so much easier than prepping fresh garlic, and it imparts all the incredible flavor of fresh garlic in every bite.

BLACK CHERRY DARK BALSAMIC VINEGAR

Even though balsamic vinegar isn't native to Greece, one of my favorite things about Greek food, especially recipes that use lamb or pork and traditional spices, is how well they lend themselves to having fruit incorporated with them. Often you won't even realize that fruity balsamic is there, but adding a touch of Black Cherry dark balsamic to a rich tomato sauce results in so much complexity and richness to the dish or sauce, it's rather unbelievable. I never tire of customers dropping by the store and mentioning that they had a dinner party the night before and used a balsamic in an unusual place—and their guests couldn't stop raving about how delicious the meal was and also couldn't figure out what the secret ingredient was.

With this rich and complex balsamic, you can do almost anything, from adding it to sauces to drizzling it straight over ice cream. It's incredibly subtle, which contributes to its versatility, but it also enhances anything it touches.

APRICOT WHITE BALSAMIC VINEGAR

This bright and fresh yet sweet balsamic is the perfect addition to so many dishes that are Greek in origin. Apricots are a very common ingredient in Greek cuisine, but it can be rather challenging—and extremely expensive—to find them, especially out of season here in North America (but easy to find in season if you're blessed to have a tree in your yard!). Introducing Apricot white balsamic vinegar into chicken or pork dishes, salad dressings, marinades, and, of course, desserts allows you to enjoy the best characteristics of apricots simply and easily. My favorite use for this balsamic is to pep up sparkling water for a refreshing drink.

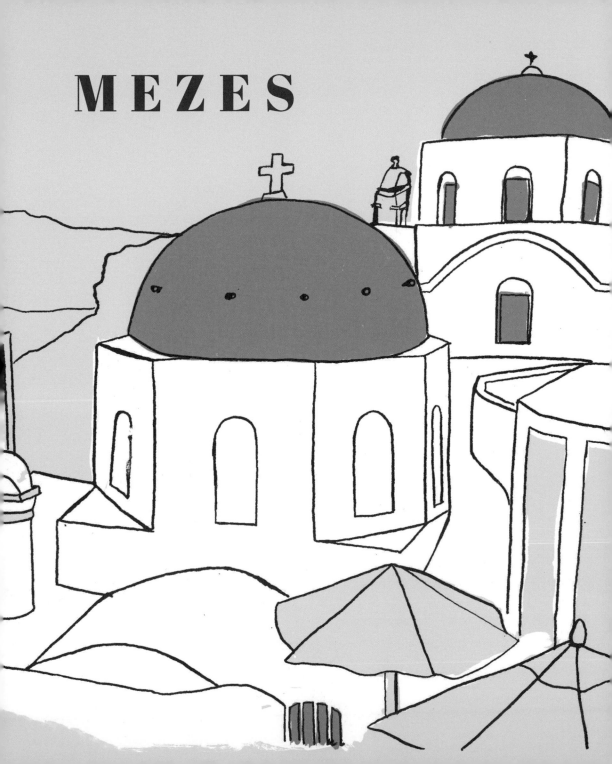

MEZES

TZATZIKI

No store-bought tzatziki comes close to the fresh, homemade version. And in addition to being cool and refreshing, this recipe keeps well. Using Garlic infused olive oil instead of fresh garlic means the garlicky taste won't increase over a few days. If you like your sauce mintier or even more refreshing, feel free to double the mint or add a drop of peppermint essential oil in addition to the mint leaves.

Place a strainer over the top of a large bowl. If the holes in your strainer are quite large, line it with a layer of cheesecloth.

Grate the cucumber. For a rustic look and slightly more chunky sauce, leave the peel on. For a cleaner, softer sauce, peel the cucumber before grating. Place the cucumber in the strainer, sprinkle with the 1 Tbsp sea salt, and toss gently to ensure the salt has been well distributed. Allow it to sit in the fridge overnight to drain. (You can weigh it down by setting a can on top of a saucer if you like, but I don't.)

Remove the cucumber from the fridge, and squeeze out any remaining liquid by pressing the cucumber down into the strainer or twisting and squeezing the cheesecloth. Transfer the cucumber to a medium-size bowl. Add the yogurt and olive oil and mix well. Roughly chop or chiffonade the mint and mix it in along with salt and pepper to taste. Garnish with an extra sprig of mint.

This will keep in an airtight container in the fridge for up to 1 week.

Serve with pita bread (page 19) and alongside Baked Feta (page 25), or as a dipping sauce for calamari (page 33), kofta, or souvlaki (page 93).

Makes 3 cups

½ seedless English cucumber

1 Tbsp sea salt

2 cups plain Greek yogurt (store-bought or homemade, see page 17)

2 Tbsp Garlic infused olive oil

6 large fresh mint leaves, stems discarded, plus 1 for garnish

Sea salt and cracked black pepper

Be sure to drain the cucumber extremely well. The less liquid you have in this dip, the better it will keep.

LEMON GARLIC HUMMUS

This hummus is extra creamy and superdelicious. The trick? Lots of olive oil and shelling the chickpeas before blending. The skin on the chickpeas creates a gritty texture that's impossible to remove once it's blended. Using Garlic infused olive oil in place of fresh garlic keeps the flavor consistent, mellow, and delicious.

————————

Drain and rinse the chickpeas, but reserve ⅓ cup of the liquid from the can.

To shell the chickpeas, gently press a chickpea between your thumb and index finger and slip it from its skin. Discard the skin and place the chickpeas in the bowl of a blender or food processor fitted with the steel blade.

Add the remaining ingredients, and blend until the hummus is smooth and creamy, scraping down the sides of the bowl a few times if necessary. If the hummus is too thick or you'd like an extra-smooth version, drizzle in the reserved chickpea liquid, continuing to blend until the desired texture is reached.

Spoon the hummus into a serving dish and use a knife to make some dips in the surface. Rather than aiming for a perfectly smooth top, drizzle some olive oil over the surface, and sprinkle with sea salt to garnish. Serve with homemade pita (page 19), crackers, or fresh veggies.

These can be stored in an airtight container in the fridge for up to 1 week.

Makes 4 cups

1 (19 oz) can chickpeas

½ cup tahini paste

¼ cup Garlic infused olive oil, plus extra for garnish

2 Tbsp lemon juice

1 tsp sea salt, plus extra for garnish

The liquid that chickpeas are stored in is called aquafaba.

HOMEMADE GREEK YOGURT

Greek yogurt is a staple in our house—couldn't be simpler to make. The only challenge is the length of time it takes to prepare and set.

————————

In a large saucepan over medium heat, heat the milk and cream just to a rolling boil, stirring constantly to prevent the mixture from burning or sticking to the bottom of the pot. (I like to use a silicone spatula for this.) Remove the pan from the heat and allow the milk mixture to cool to slightly warmer than lukewarm (110°F–115°F). This temperature is important; if the milk is too hot, it will kill the bacteria, and if it's too cold, the bacteria won't be activated and your yogurt won't set.

While you're waiting for the milk to cool, place a clean casserole dish (about 4-cup capacity) in the oven and preheat the oven to 300°F. When it reaches temperature, turn it off.

When the milk has cooled, whisk in the yogurt until fully incorporated. Remove the casserole dish from the oven, pour in the milk mixture, put on the lid, and place in the warm oven. The warmed oven and casserole dish will hold their heat and allow the yogurt to set. Leave the yogurt in the oven for 6–8 hours, or overnight.

Remove the casserole dish from the oven. The yogurt will jiggle slightly when moved, and you'll notice a bit of surface water that's separated from the yogurt. For a creamy yogurt, whisk the water into the yogurt. For an extra-thick yogurt, spoon it into a cheesecloth-lined strainer placed over a bowl and let it sit, uncovered, in the fridge for 3–4 hours.

Gently whisk the olive oil into the yogurt. Spoon it into clean mason jars with airtight lids, and store in the fridge for 3–4 days.

Makes 3 cups, plus enough starter for the next batch

2 cups whole milk

1 cup heavy (35%) cream

¾ cup Greek yogurt with live bacterial cultures

2 Tbsp Lemon fused olive oil

Once you start making yogurt, make sure you always reserve ¾ cup of the yogurt for the next batch, keeping the bacterial cultures alive.

————

If you want a plain Greek yogurt, simply use extra virgin olive oil in place of the oils I've used here.

FRESH HOMEMADE PITA BREAD

Pita is so versatile. It can be used for wraps, sandwiches, pizza crusts, scooping up a delightful hummus, or sopping up the residue of soup or stew. And homemade pita, nice and toasty warm, fresh out of the oven? Simply amazing. This recipe is easily doubled or tripled, so you can prep extra and pop them in the freezer for future meals.

In a small saucepan over medium heat, heat the water and 2 Tbsp of the olive oil to very warm (about 110°F).

Preheat the oven to 200°F. As soon as it reaches temperature, turn it off.

In a large mixing bowl, mix together the flour, sugar, yeast, and salt. Make a well in the flour mixture and slowly pour in the warm water. Mix thoroughly to form a soft, sticky dough.

Turn the dough out onto a lightly floured surface and knead it for 8–10 minutes, until smooth and elastic. Drizzle a few tablespoons of the remaining olive oil into a large bowl, place the dough in the bowl, and turn to coat it evenly. Cover with a dry tea towel and place it in the oven to rise for 20 minutes.

Line a baking tray with parchment paper.

Remove the risen dough from the oven, place it on a lightly floured surface, divide it into eight equal pieces, and roll each piece into a ball. Place the dough balls on the baking tray and drizzle each with a little olive oil. Rub in the oil well to ensure the dough doesn't dry out. Drape a slightly damp clean towel loosely over the top and let rest in a warm, draft-free spot for 5 minutes.

Preheat the oven to 500°F, or as hot as your oven will go, and place a baking sheet or pizza stone in it to preheat as well.

Makes 8 pita breads

1 cup water

6 Tbsp Garlic infused olive oil, divided, plus extra for frying

2 cups all-purpose flour, plus extra for kneading

2 Tbsp granulated sugar

1 Tbsp quick-rising yeast

1 tsp sea salt

Meanwhile, on a lightly floured surface, roll out each pita ball to about 6–7 inches wide, flipping it over as you roll to prevent sticking, then lay each pita back on the lined baking tray in a single layer. (You can make pitas in batches.) Be careful not to tear the dough or it won't puff properly when baking. Cover with a slightly damp clean towel and let rise in a warm, draft-free spot for about 20 minutes.

Drizzle a little olive oil into a heavy-bottomed frying pan over high heat.

Lay two pitas, evenly spaced, on the hot baking sheet or pizza stone and bake for 2–3 minutes, until they puff up and are lightly brown. Remove the pitas from the oven and cook in the frying pan for 30 seconds to 1 minute to lightly char them. Repeat with the remaining pitas. Store them wrapped in a towel, or allow to cool and transfer to an airtight container. These will keep for 1–2 days at room temperature, 1 week in the fridge, or up to 3 months in the freezer.

These will go soggy if placed in an airtight container before they're completely cool, so give them plenty of time to cool down.

TOMATO and KALAMATA FLATBREAD

This simple flatbread is a great appetizer for a movie night or a feast—and it's easily doubled or tripled for a crowd. The Garlic infused olive oil in the dough and on top ensures you'll have delicious garlicky flavor in every bite!

In a large bowl, whisk together the flour, sugar, yeast, and salt until fully combined. Create a well in the middle of the flour mixture.

In a small saucepan over medium heat, heat the water to 110°F. Add it to the flour mixture along with ¼ cup of the olive oil. Mix well to form a soft, sticky dough. Turn the dough onto a lightly floured surface and knead until smooth and elastic, 8–10 minutes.

Place 2 Tbsp of the olive oil in a medium bowl and place the dough in the bowl, turning it to coat it evenly with oil. Cover with a dry tea towel and set it in a warm, draft-free place to rise for 10 minutes.

While the dough is rising, roughly chop the tomato, shallot, parsley, and oregano. Add 2 Tbsp olive oil and chopped herbs and veggies into the blender. Pulse to form a chunky mixture.

Preheat the oven to 450°F. Line a baking tray with parchment paper. Roll out the dough to a ½-inch-thick oval or rectangle on a lightly floured surface.

Place the dough on the prepared baking tray. Brush with the remaining 2 Tbsp of olive oil, and let rest, uncovered, for a few minutes in a warm place, while you chop the olives. Gently brush the tomato mixture over the dough, right to the edges, and scatter the olives over the top.

Bake for 8–10 minutes, until the edges are golden and the center is firm, not doughy. Remove from the oven, and cut and serve immediately. This can be stored in an airtight container in the fridge for up to 3 days.

SERVES
FOUR

2 cups all-purpose flour, plus extra for dusting

1 Tbsp granulated sugar

1 tsp quick-rising yeast

1 tsp sea salt

¾ cup water

½ cup + 2 Tbsp Garlic infused olive oil, divided

1 large on-the-vine tomato

1 shallot

1 Tbsp chopped fresh curly-leaf parsley

1 Tbsp fresh oregano leaves

½ cup Kalamata olives, pitted

BAKED FETA

This is one of my favorite appetizers. Warm and delicious, it's great before almost any meal. The tangy feta and sweet roasted tomatoes are a perfect match for crackers, crusty bread, or pita (page 19). From a movie-night snack to part of a crowd of appies, this dish will always please.

———————

Preheat the oven to 375°F.

Slice the tomatoes and olives in half, roughly chop the onion, and add them all to a mixing bowl. Drizzle in the olive oil and lemon juice and sprinkle with the seasonings. Toss to evenly coat.

Line a small baking tray or shallow baking dish with parchment paper. Place the block of feta in the middle of the paper. Top the feta with the tomato mixture, piling it high and allowing some to fall to the side. Scrape out the bowl that the tomato mixture was in, drizzling any residue oil and seasonings over the top of everything.

Bake, uncovered, for 20 minutes, until the tomatoes are starting to caramelize and the feta has softened. Feta cheese doesn't melt, but as it warms, it softens and becomes spreadable. Serve warm with pita (page 19), crackers, or fresh crusty bread.

This can be stored in an airtight container in the fridge for up to 3 days.

SERVES
FOUR-SIX
———

1 cup cherry tomatoes
½ cup Kalamata olives, pitted
¼ small red onion
¼ cup Garlic infused olive oil
2 tsp lemon juice
2 tsp chopped fresh oregano leaves
1 tsp sea salt
½ tsp cracked black pepper
1 lb block feta cheese

SAGANAKI

Is there anything better than gooey warm cheese? How about gooey warm cheese *set on fire*? I bring you saganaki.

If you bought your cheese as a block, rather than in a one long slice, cut it into ¾-inch-thick slices and repeat the steps below for each slice.

Pour the water into a shallow dish. Place the flour in a separate dish and add salt and pepper to taste.

Brush both sides of the cheese with 1 Tbsp of the olive oil, then dredge in flour, shaking off any excess. Place the cheese gently in the water, turning to coat, then place it in the flour, turning again to ensure it's well coated and well floured.

Heat the remaining 3 Tbsp of olive oil over medium-high heat in a heavy-bottomed frying pan. Add the cheese (you may need to work in batches if you had to slice your cheese) and fry for 2 minutes per side to form a beautiful golden crust around the cheese.

Immediately before serving and while it's still in the frying pan, add the brandy and use a lighter to set the cheese on fire. Squeeze a lemon wedge over the top to put out the fire. Serve with pita (page 19), crackers, or fresh crusty bread and lemon wedges.

This is best consumed immediately, as leftovers don't keep or reheat very well.

8 oz saganaki cheese
½ cup water
½ cup all-purpose flour
Sea salt and cracked black pepper
4 Tbsp Lemon fused olive oil
2 Tbsp brandy
Lemon wedges

SPINACH PIE

Simple, delicious, and infinitely versatile, this spinach pie sustained me through my university career, and I still make it every week. It makes the perfect breakfast—packed with greens and protein served with a dollop of Greek yogurt (page 17) and toast—a slice is easily transported almost anywhere for lunch, or enjoy it for dinner alongside Lemon Rice Soup (page 44). The Garlic infused olive oil adds lots of flavor to the fresh herbs and prevents the garlic from overwhelming the flavors of the other ingredients.

––––––––––––––

Preheat the oven to 350°F. Grease a 9-inch pie plate with extra virgin olive oil and set aside.

In a large mixing bowl, whisk together the eggs, yogurt, milk and ¼ cup of the olive oil to form a smooth, creamy mixture. If there are a few lumps from the yogurt, that's OK. Set aside.

Heat the remaining ¼ cup olive oil in a large frying pan over medium heat. Roughly chop the onion and sauté it in the olive oil for 3–4 minutes, until soft. Add salt and pepper to sweat the onions. Gently tear up the spinach into small pieces and add it to the pan in batches, stirring between additions so the spinach wilts. When all the spinach has been added, add the fresh herbs and sauté until all the greens are wilted and the onion is very tender.

Transfer the spinach mixture into the prepared baking dish, spreading it so it evenly covers the dish. Gently pour the egg mixture over the greens until it's within ½ inch of the top of the dish. Top with the crumbled feta cheese.

Bake for 35–40 minutes, until a knife inserted in the center of the pie comes out clean and the top is golden brown. Remove from the oven and immediately run a knife around the outside before cutting into slices to serve.

SERVES
SIX

6 eggs

¾ cup plain Greek yogurt (store-bought or homemade, see page 17)

½ cup 2% milk

½ cup Garlic infused olive oil, divided

1 large red onion

Sea salt and cracked black pepper

6 cups fresh baby spinach, stems discarded

½ cup fresh curly-leaf parsley, chopped

¼ cup fresh dill, chopped

1 cup crumbled feta cheese

KEFTEDES

The mixture of pork and beef gives these meatballs great flavor and texture, and the Lemon fused olive oil and Apricot white balsamic vinegar work with the flavors of the meat to create a unique and delicious flavor profile.

Line a baking tray with parchment paper. Place paper towel underneath a wire rack.

Place the onion and bread crumbs in the bowl of a food processor fitted with the steel blade and process finely. Add the beef and pork and pulse to ensure the meat is well broken up. Add the eggs, olive oil, and balsamic and continue to pulse until the mixture is stiff.

Place this mixture in a large mixing bowl and add the parsley and mint. Using your hands, mix everything to ensure all the ingredients are well combined.

Using a small scoop or teaspoon measure, spoon a small amount of the meat into your hand and form 1-inch meatballs. Sift the cornstarch into a mixing bowl. Roll each meatball gently in the cornstarch to coat and then place them on the prepared baking tray. Transfer to the fridge and leave, uncovered, for 1 hour to chill.

Heat ½ inch of olive oil in the bottom of a large frying pan over medium heat. Add the meatballs, working in batches so you don't overcrowd the pan. Cook for 3–5 minutes, turning the meatballs to ensure they're well browned on all sides. Place them on the wire rack for 2–3 minutes to drain off any excess oil, and then cut open one or two meatballs per batch to ensure they're all well done. Serve warm with toothpicks or with a side of tzatziki (page 13) as an appetizer, or for lunch with Lemon Roasted Potatoes (page 117) and fresh veggies.

Makes 36 small meatballs

1 small red onion

¾ cup dried bread crumbs

½ lb ground beef

½ lb ground pork

2 eggs

1 Tbsp Lemon fused olive oil

1 Tbsp Apricot white balsamic vinegar

¼ cup finely chopped fresh curly-leaf parsley

1 Tbsp finely chopped fresh mint leaves

½ cup cornstarch

Extra virgin olive oil for frying

As you're rolling the meatballs, do your best to ensure they don't have any seams and are completely smooth on the outside—this will prevent them from splitting open when frying.

CALAMARI

I prefer to make calamari at home where I can ensure the freshness of the squid and how quickly it's cooked—that's what will make or break this dish.

Thaw the squid (if you're using frozen), rinse well, and pat dry with paper towel. Separate the pieces and, using a sharp knife, cut the body from the base of the neck and the tentacles, removing the head from the center. Cut the body into parallel strips, forming the rings. Carefully feel at the base of the tentacles and, using a sharp knife again, remove the beaks.

In a medium-size bowl, toss the dry squid with the olive oil and then set aside in the fridge until needed.

In a separate bowl, whisk together the flour, cornstarch, and seasonings until well combined. Add the oiled squid and toss gently to coat, ensuring all the pieces are well coated. Gently transfer the squid to a resealable plastic bag and lay it flat in the fridge until ready to serve (2–3 hours is fine, but absolutely no longer than 12).

Place paper towel under a wire rack.

Heat 3–4 inches of oil in a heavy-bottomed saucepan to 375°F. The oil needs to be deep enough for the squid to be completely submerged. When the oil has reached temperature, gently add the squid. Fry it for no longer than 2 minutes. It will be lightly golden and crisp. Using a slotted spoon, remove the calamari from the hot oil and place it on the prepared wire rack to let the excess oil drip off.

Transfer to a serving dish and enjoy immediately. Serve with tzatziki (page 13) for a dipping sauce or with a squeeze of lemon over the top. This is best consumed immediately as leftovers don't keep or reheat well.

1 lb fresh (or frozen and thawed) squid tubes and tentacles, cleaned

2 Tbsp Garlic infused olive oil

½ cup all-purpose flour

¼ cup cornstarch

1 tsp sea salt

½ tsp cracked black pepper

½ tsp dried oregano

½ tsp smoked paprika

3–4 cups mild-flavored oil for deep-frying

The fresher the squid, the better. If you don't live close to the ocean, I recommend purchasing frozen squid, as it is typically flash-frozen and will be much fresher than something that's been sitting on ice for a few days while traveling to the supermarket.

SPANAKOPITA PUFFS

Is it wrong to struggle with loving phyllo pastry? I find it temperamental, not very flavorful, and messy to eat. However, I do love spanakopita with its combination of tangy feta, bittersweet onion, and creamy spinach housed in a pastry crust. What to do? Enter puff pastry. It allows all the best qualities of all the ingredients to shine, adds simplicity, and takes away anything that could possibly detract from this perfect dish.

Preheat the oven to 350°F. Line a baking tray with parchment paper.

On a floured surface, gently roll out each piece of puff pastry into a 12- × 12-inch square. Cover with a slightly damp tea towel and set aside at room temperature until needed.

Dice the onion and add it to a frying pan with the olive oil over medium heat. Sauté the onion until soft, 2–3 minutes, then sprinkle in the sea salt and stir again.

Gently tear up the spinach into small pieces and add it to the pan in batches, stirring between additions so the spinach wilts. When all the spinach has been added, sauté for 2–3 more minutes, until the spinach is soft and tender. Pour in the cream, add the pepper and nutmeg, and continue to stir, still over medium (or medium-high) heat, until the cream thickens, about 5 minutes. Remove from the heat and transfer to a bowl. Add the feta cheese and mix well to combine.

Using a sharp knife or pizza cutter, cut the puff pastry into nine squares. In the center of each square, place a generous tablespoon of the spinach mixture. Gently brush the edges of the pastry with water and pull the points together at the top, making a little pocket.

SERVES
FOUR

1 (8 oz) package (2 squares) frozen puff pastry, thawed

1 small yellow onion

2 Tbsp Garlic infused olive oil

1 tsp sea salt

6 cups fresh baby spinach, stems discarded

½ cup heavy (35%) cream

½ tsp cracked black pepper

Pinch of freshly grated or ground nutmeg

¾ cup crumbled feta cheese

If your brand of puff pastry comes as one block and not two, cut it in half before proceeding.

Place each pocket on the prepared baking tray, about 2 inches apart. Repeat with the second rectangle of puff pastry and remaining spinach mixture.

Bake for 15 minutes, until golden and puffed. Serve immediately.

These can be stored in an airtight container in the fridge for up to 3 days. They don't reheat well, though, so you might prefer to enjoy leftovers cold. If you do decide to reheat them, pop them in a paper bag and warm them up for 10–15 minutes in a warm, not hot, oven.

CARROT, LEEK, and ZUCCHINI FRITTERS

Fritters are so versatile and easy to incorporate into almost any setting. These are a delightful, savory breakfast addition—think veggie-loaded pancake, topped with a poached egg, some extra feta, and hollandaise if you're so inclined. Frying them in the Garlic infused olive oil gives them a lovely flavor that permeates every bite.

Line a large strainer with a layer of cheesecloth and set it over a large bowl. Place the grated zucchini in the strainer, sprinkle with salt, and place it in the fridge for 10–15 minutes to allow the zucchini to drain. (You can place a saucer on top with a weight to press down on the zucchini if you like, but I just give the cheesecloth a good squeeze after a few minutes.)

Meanwhile, in a large mixing bowl, whisk together the eggs and olive oil. Add the flour, cornstarch, and baking powder, whisking to form a thick, lump-free batter. Add a bit of milk if the batter seems dry.

Add the leek, carrot, parsley, mint, feta, and salt and pepper to taste.

Remove the zucchini from the fridge, press down on it to remove any extra water, then pull up the sides of the cheesecloth and squeeze the zucchini even more to drain off all the excess liquid.

Add the zucchini to the batter and mix well to completely coat the vegetables in the batter mixture.

In a heavy-bottomed frying pan over medium heat, heat some olive oil. Spoon between 2 Tbsp and ¼ cup of the fritter batter into the warm pan. Add 2–3 more fritters to the pan, being careful not to overcrowd it. Fry the fritters for 2 minutes per side, until golden, bubbling, and cooked through. Serve warm or chilled with tzatziki (page 13) on the side for dipping.

SERVES
FOUR-SIX

2 cups grated zucchini
(skin on, scrubbed)

1 Tbsp sea salt

2 eggs

2 Tbsp Garlic infused olive oil,
plus extra for frying

½ cup all-purpose flour

½ cup cornstarch

1 tsp baking powder

1 leek, finely sliced

1 cup grated carrot

½ cup chopped fresh
curly-leaf parsley

½ cup chopped fresh mint leaves

½ cup crumbled feta

Sea salt and cracked black pepper

GIGANDES PLAKI (BAKED BUTTER BEANS)

Hearty and fulfilling, it's no wonder that beans are a big part of the Greek diet—and mine too. These baked butter beans are the perfect afternoon snack with a dollop of Greek yogurt (page 17), served as an appetizer with pita (page 19) to sop up all their goodness, or as a side with a light brunch or lunch. Make lots and make this often.

———————————

In a saucepan over medium heat, sauté the chopped onion in the olive oil until the onion is just translucent. Add the sea salt and continue to cook, stirring, to sweat the onions for 3–4 minutes, just until they start to brown. Add the vinegar and scrape the bottom of the pan to deglaze it. Gently pour in the juice from the tomatoes, and increase the heat to bring the juice to a boil. Either gently add the tomatoes one at a time (to avoid splashing), or slowly crush each one in your hand before adding to the juice mixture. Once all the tomatoes have been added, stir continuously to break them up, 2–3 minutes.

Add the beans to the tomato mixture. Turn down the heat to low and simmer, uncovered, for 15–20 minutes, until the tomato sauce has thickened and the beans are soft. Serve warm.

These beans will keep in an airtight container in the fridge for up to 2 weeks.

SERVES
SIX

Makes 4 cups

1 large yellow onion,
finely chopped

½ cup Garlic infused olive oil

1 tsp sea salt

2 Tbsp red wine vinegar

1 (28 oz) can plum tomatoes

2 (19 oz) cans butter beans,
drained and rinsed

Sea salt and cracked black pepper

If you have a hard time finding butter beans, then cannellini or white kidney beans will do the trick! I've even used black and navy beans in a pinch. The key is to use beans with a soft skin (not red kidney beans, for example) so they spread easily and soak up all the flavor.

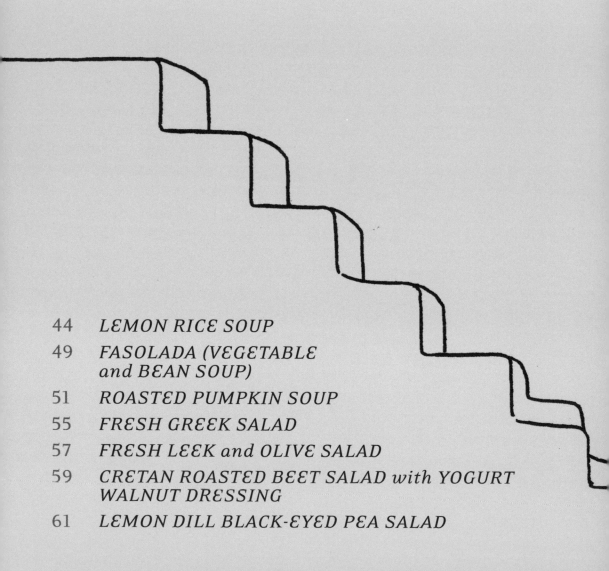

SOUPS
&
SALADS

LEMON RICE SOUP

This creamy soup is refreshing and hearty in every way. It's also dairy-free—the lovely creamy texture comes from whisking the egg yolks and lemon juice together, rather than using cream. Fresh herbs are lovely as a garnish, and sometimes I'll top this with feta (although that does take the dairy-free piece out of the picture, of course). Sautéing the onions and rice in the Lemon fused olive oil ensures that the lemon flavor is imparted into the entire recipe and not only into the creamy sauce mixture that's added at the end. This gives the soup a really round and full lemon flavor rather than a sharp lemon bite—it's warming and refreshing all at the same time.

———————————

In a large stockpot over medium heat, bring the stock and saffron to a simmer and then turn the heat down to low.

Mince the onion very finely—the goal is for the onion pieces to be the size of a grain of rice.

In a heavy-bottomed saucepan over medium heat, heat the oil and then add the onion. Sauté for 2 minutes, until soft but not browned, and then add the rice, parsley, dill, and salt and pepper to taste. Stir well to coat the rice in the olive oil and sauté, still stirring, for 2–3 minutes, until the rice is translucent. Slowly add the stock to the saucepan, bring it to a rolling boil, then turn down the heat, cover with a lid, and simmer for 25–30 minutes, or until the rice is tender. From this point on, do not place the lid on the pot—this will ensure the egg doesn't separate after it has been added.

In a separate bowl, whisk the egg yolks and lemon juice together until they're light and creamy in texture. As you continue to whisk, gently ladle 1–2 Tbsp of stock off the top of the soup into the egg mixture. Continue adding stock, 2 Tbsp at a time until you've added ½ cup in total,

SERVES
FOUR

4 cups chicken or vegetable stock

4–5 strands of saffron

1 small red onion

¼ cup Lemon fused olive oil

¾ cup uncooked short-grain rice

¼ cup chopped fresh curly-leaf parsley, plus a few sprigs for garnish

2 Tbsp chopped fresh dill

Sea salt and cracked black pepper

3 egg yolks

¼ cup lemon juice (about 2 lemons)

Remember: after the egg mixture has been added, you mustn't cover the soup, even if you're only reheating it. The eggs may separate and curdle.

to temper the yolks. Once the yolks are warm and the mixture is starting to thicken slightly (it should coat the back of a spoon), start to whisk in a very fine stream into the saucepan. Stirring constantly over medium heat, bring the soup to a simmer but not to a boil, 5–8 minutes. The soup will start to thicken and be very creamy. Remove from the heat and serve immediately.

This can be stored in an airtight container in the fridge for up to 2 days.

FASOLADA (VEGETABLE and BEAN SOUP)

This soup, a simple bean soup, is often called the Greek national dish. It's best made in large batches and enjoyed throughout the week. Actually, it hits peak taste on Day Three, when the flavors have had a chance to really meld together. There are hundreds of variations on this recipe, and every family has their own favorite. Traditionally, it's made with dried beans, but I've used canned beans here to speed things up.

In the bottom of a large soup pot over medium-high heat, heat the olive oil. Add the onions and sauté for 5–10 minutes, until just translucent. Add salt and pepper to taste and stir for 2–3 minutes. Add the carrots and celery and sauté for 5 minutes, until the onions are just starting to brown.

Add the beans and then the stock to the pot. Bring to a boil, turn down the heat to medium-low, and simmer, covered, for 35 minutes, until the carrots are tender and cooked through. This is particularly wonderful with fresh crusty bread on a cold winter day.

This will keep in an airtight container in the fridge for up to 3 days.

SERVES
EIGHT

½ cup Garlic infused olive oil

1 large red onion, diced

Sea salt and cracked black pepper

2 medium carrots, peeled and roughly chopped

2 stalks celery, roughly chopped

4 large on-the-vine tomatoes

2 (19 oz) cans navy beans, drained and rinsed

1 (19 oz) can white kidney beans, drained and rinsed

8 cups vegetable stock

ROASTED PUMPKIN SOUP

Pumpkin is a very common vegetable in Greece—something I didn't realize until I was digging around some traditional Greek cookbooks. It's used in savory dishes such as soups and stews where North Americans might use a squash, and it's also superdelicious simply roasted and presented as a side dish. In this simple soup recipe, roasting the pumpkin in the Lemon fused olive oil brings out a touch of sweetness without overpowering the other flavors.

———————————

Preheat the oven to 400°F.

Slice the pumpkin in half, remove the seeds (setting them aside for now), and place the pumpkin cut side down directly on the oven rack. (You might want to place a baking tray directly underneath to catch any cooking juices.) Bake for 45 minutes.

Leaving their skin on, slice the onions in half widthwise and place them on a baking tray. Slice the top off the head of garlic, keeping the skin on and the bulb otherwise intact, and add it to the baking tray.

Remove the pumpkin from the oven and place it cut side up on the baking tray.

Drizzle the head of garlic and onions with a few tablespoons of the olive oil, then use the remaining olive oil to brush the cut sides of the pumpkin. Scatter the paprika and cumin over the top of all the veggies, and season to taste with salt and pepper. Bake for 20 minutes and then remove from the oven and allow to cool enough to handle.

In a large soup pot over medium-high heat, squeeze the garlic from the bulb, scrape the flesh from the roasted pumpkin, and add the onions (without the skin) and any cooking juices, and pour in the vegetable stock. Bring to a

SERVES
FOUR
———

1 small pumpkin (see sidebar)

2 yellow onions

1 head of garlic

½ cup Lemon fused olive oil, divided, plus extra for garnish

1 tsp smoked paprika

½ tsp ground cumin

Sea salt and cracked black pepper

4 cups vegetable stock

1½ cups plain Greek yogurt (store-bought or homemade, see page 17), divided

Toasted pumpkin seeds for garnish

boil, then turn down the heat to medium-low and simmer, covered, for 25 minutes.

Remove from the heat and let cool, uncovered, for 10 minutes. In batches, transfer the soup to a food processor fitted with the steel blade or a blender, and purée until creamy smooth. Return to the pot, and place over the lowest possible heat. Whisk in 1 cup of the Greek yogurt. Simmer for 5 minutes to ensure the soup is warmed all the way through. Transfer to serving bowls and serve with a dollop of the remaining yogurt and pumpkin seeds scattered over the top.

Leftover soup can be stored in an airtight container in the fridge for up to 3 days, or frozen for up to 3 months.

A small pumpkin will weigh 3–5 lb fresh and yield 2½–4 lb of cooked pumpkin—that's 3–4 cups of puréed pumpkin, or the equivalent of about two (14 oz) cans of pumpkin purée. Smaller, baby pumpkins are often called pie pumpkins or sugar pumpkins and have a lovely creamy texture and sweet taste when cooked. Larger pumpkins cook up more like a butternut squash and are quite stringy and tarter than the smaller, sweeter varieties.

The most important thing to remember when baking a whole pumpkin? Save the seeds! Wash them well, and soak them for 12 hours in ½ cup Apricot white balsamic vinegar, 2 Tbsp sea salt, and enough water to just cover them, then drain and pat dry. Drizzle with 2–3 Tbsp of extra virgin olive oil and 1 tsp of sea salt and any other spices you like (cumin and smoked paprika, or cinnamon and nutmeg for a sweeter version), and roast in a 325°F oven for 45 minutes– 1 hour, shaking and turning about halfway through, until golden brown and well toasted.

FRESH GREEK SALAD

A colorful Greek salad is one of my favorite sides. It always makes me think of summer no matter the weather, with its bright yellow and red tomatoes, lovely green cucumber, and chunks of feta, all dripping in olive oil. Traditionally you would use a robust extra virgin olive oil and red wine vinegar. I've used Garlic infused olive oil as I love a garlicky pop in every bite of salad. It's also delicious with Lemon fused olive oil and Black Cherry dark balsamic vinegar.

In a large bowl, whisk together the olive oil, vinegar, lemon juice and zest, oregano, and salt and pepper to taste.

Chop the tomatoes and cucumber, thinly slice the onion, and add them all to the bowl. Toss to coat in the dressing mixture. Top with feta, carefully crumbling it a bit more but still leaving large chunks, and olives. Gently toss to coat with dressing, top with some fresh oregano, and enjoy!

This can be stored in an airtight container in the fridge for up to 3 days.

SERVES
FOUR

¼ cup Garlic infused olive oil

1 Tbsp red wine vinegar

1 Tbsp lemon juice

Zest of 1 lemon

1 Tbsp chopped fresh oregano leaves, plus extra for garnish

Sea salt and cracked black pepper

2 cups cherry tomatoes, a variety of colors

1 English cucumber, skin on

1 small red onion

1 cup Kalamata olives

2 cups roughly crumbled feta cheese

Fresh oregano leaves for garnish

FRESH LEEK and OLIVE SALAD

This salad originates from the north of Greece and shows off the olive oil from the region perfectly. Fresh, tart, and bright, thanks in part to the tangy sweet Apricot white balsamic vinegar, this salad is just as lovely as soon as it's made as it is a day later, after the flavors have had a chance to mellow and soften. The balsamic brightens the natural flavor of the fruit and adds complexity and depth. After the fruit has had a chance to marinate in the dressing, the flavor deepens and softens, adding a unique slant to the salad.

SERVES
FOUR

4 leeks

2 tsp sea salt

¼ cup extra virgin olive oil

2 Tbsp Apricot white balsamic vinegar

1 cup Kalamata olives, pitted

Wash the leeks well and cut off the green leaves, leaving only the white parts. Using a mandolin, slices the leeks into a large bowl. Sprinkle with the sea salt and allow to sit for 4–5 minutes to soften slightly.

Drizzle in the olive oil and balsamic, and gently toss to evenly coat.

Slice the olives in half and add them to the leeks. Place the salad in the fridge, covered, for at least 1 hour before serving.

This can be stored in an airtight container in the fridge for up to 3 days.

SOUPS & SALADS   **57**

CRETAN ROASTED BEET SALAD
with YOGURT WALNUT DRESSING

This salad is amazing any time of year. I serve it warm as a side in winter with the yogurt as a dip on the side, and as a potato-style salad in summer, chilled and tossed in the yogurt. If I'm feeling adventurous, I'll make this with a combination of golden beets and red sugar beets—keeping them separate until serving time, of course, so the colors don't run together.

Wash the beets and slice the tops and ends off.

Bring a large pot of water to a boil over medium heat and cook the beets until fork-tender, 30–45 minutes. Drain and allow to become cool enough to handle.

Preheat the oven to 375°F. Line a baking tray with parchment paper.

Peel the beets and cut them into wedges. Place them on the prepared baking tray and drizzle with 2 Tbsp of the oil and ¼ cup of the balsamic. Toss well to ensure the beets are well coated. Sprinkle with salt and pepper to taste and roast in the oven for 15–18 minutes, until the beets are caramelized and the edges are starting to crisp.

In a small frying pan over medium heat, place the walnuts. Dry-toast the walnuts until they're just browning and releasing a lovely toasted scent, 3–4 minutes. Remove from the heat and set aside.

While the beets are roasting, whisk together the remaining 2 Tbsp oil, 1 Tbsp balsamic, and yogurt. Add salt and pepper to taste. Remove the beets from the oven and allow to cool slightly.

To serve warm, transfer the beets to a large mixing bowl, top with the yogurt dressing, and toss gently to coat. The yogurt will turn a lovely pink color. Divide the salad between individual serving places and top each one with ¼ cup chopped walnuts.

SERVES
FOUR

2 lb beets

¼ cup Lemon fused olive oil, divided

¼ cup + 1 Tbsp Apricot white balsamic vinegar

Sea salt and cracked black pepper

1 cup chopped untoasted walnuts

1 cup plain Greek yogurt (store-bought or homemade, see page 17)

To serve cold, allow the beets to cool completely. Place the yogurt dressing in a small serving dish, top with the walnuts, and place in the middle of a large serving plate. Arrange the beets on the serving plate around the dish of dressing.

The salad and dressing can be stored in separate airtight containers in the fridge for up to 3 days.

LEMON DILL BLACK-EYED PEA SALAD

This simple everyday salad is hearty and versatile. Try adding roasted red peppers for more color or chilies for added spice, or switching out the black-eyed peas for chickpeas. The Garlic infused olive oil creates a delicious, even flavor that doesn't dominate the rest of the dish. I often make this as a quick and easy lunch, or as a side salad for a picnic.

1 (19 oz) can black-eyed peas
2 Tbsp Garlic infused olive oil
Juice and grated zest of 1 lemon
½ cup chopped fresh dill
Sea salt and cracked black pepper

Drain and rinse the black-eyed peas and place them in a medium-size bowl. Drizzle with the olive oil and lemon juice and toss to coat. Add the dill, season with salt and pepper to taste, and toss gently to coat again.

Top with the lemon zest and serve. You can eat this immediately or let it sit in the fridge for a few hours to let the flavors develop.

This will keep in an airtight container in the fridge for up to 3 days.

MAINS

MOUSSAKA

If there was ever a classic Greek main dish, this is it. It combines all the traditional flavors, spices, vegetables, and sauces of the Greek islands into one amazingly tasty dish. It can take a bit of time to prepare, but each component can also be prepared separately and then assembled later, so don't be put off trying this. I tend to make it for dinner on a Sunday night, and it turns into the perfect Monday lunch! The Black Cherry dark balsamic vinegar adds a rich and sweet, almost molasses note to the ground beef and sauce. This, in tandem with the Garlic infused olive oil, ensures that the dish is extra flavorful and well balanced, and not too greasy.

Grease a 9- × 13-inch baking dish with extra virgin olive oil. Place a layer of paper towel under a wire rack. Line a baking tray with parchment paper.

To prepare the vegetable filling, slice the eggplant and zucchini into ¼-inch-thick rounds and place them in one even layer on the prepared wire rack. Sprinkle with ½ Tbsp of the salt, then flip the pieces over, sprinkle with the remaining ½ Tbsp of salt, and let rest for 30 minutes to allow the water to seep out. Preheat the oven to 400°F. Pat the slices dry with fresh paper towel. Transfer the vegetables to the prepared baking tray and drizzle with the olive oil. Sprinkle with pepper to taste and roast in the oven for 15–20 minutes, until the vegetables are just soft, then turn them over and roast for 10 more minutes. Remove from the oven and set aside to cool.

To prepare the meat sauce, in a large saucepan over medium-high heat, brown the ground beef or lamb. Use a wooden spoon to break the meat into small pieces, 3–5 minutes. Add the onions and garlic and sauté for 3–5 minutes, until the onions are soft. Drain off

SERVES
SIX-EIGHT

Vegetable Filling

1 large eggplant, skin on

1 large zucchini, skin on

1 Tbsp sea salt, divided

¼ cup Garlic infused olive oil

Cracked black pepper

Meat Sauce

1 lb ground beef or lamb

1 medium red onion, chopped

4 garlic cloves, finely chopped

2 Tbsp Black Cherry dark balsamic vinegar

1 cup dry red wine

1 tsp ground cinnamon

¼ tsp ground allspice

1 (14 oz) can whole tomatoes, with juice

1 (5½ oz) can tomato paste

Béchamel Sauce

¼ cup Garlic infused olive oil

¼ cup all-purpose flour

1 cup 2% milk

1 cup heavy (35%) cream

2 egg yolks

Pinch of freshly grated or ground nutmeg

Sea salt

1 cup freshly grated Parmesan cheese, divided

excess fat from the meat, then pour in the balsamic and
red wine, scraping bits from the bottom of the pan back
up into the meat and onion mixture. Cook for 5–7 minutes,
stirring constantly, to allow the sauce to reduce slightly.
Sprinkle the cinnamon and allspice over the meat, stirring
well to ensure everything is fully combined. Gently pour
in the juice from the canned tomatoes, then gently crush
the tomatoes into your hand and add them to the pan,
one at a time to avoid splashing. Continue to sauté for
3–5 minutes, until the meat sauce reaches a gentle boil.
Stir in the tomato paste, stirring continuously for about 10
minutes until it forms a thick sauce. Turn down the heat
to low and simmer, uncovered, for 30 minutes to let the
sauce continue to thicken, stirring occasionally to prevent
sticking. Remove from the heat and set aside.

While the sauce simmers, prepare the béchamel
sauce. First, heat the olive oil in a nonstick saucepan (you
need nonstick for this recipe) over medium heat. Whisk in
the flour. It will bubble up and foam, then reduce down
to a creamy paste. Add 3–4 Tbsp of the milk, stirring
continuously. Still stirring, slowly add the remaining milk
and then the cream. Once all of the cream has been
added, remove the pan from the heat. Whisk in the egg
yolks, nutmeg, and salt to taste. When the mixture is fully
combined, add ¾ cup of the Parmesan cheese.

Preheat the oven to 350°F.

To assemble the moussaka, in the bottom of the
prepared pan, arrange an even layer of eggplant and
zucchini slices. Top with an even layer of meat sauce, then
a second layer of eggplant and zucchini. I tend to place
the eggplant first, then use the smaller slices of zucchini to
fill in the gaps. Repeat until all the vegetables and meat
sauce have been used. I usually get about three layers,
but it depends on how large the vegetables are and how

For a veggie option, substitute
1 cup of crumbled feta cheese
plus 1 cup of grated mozzarella
cheese for the beef.

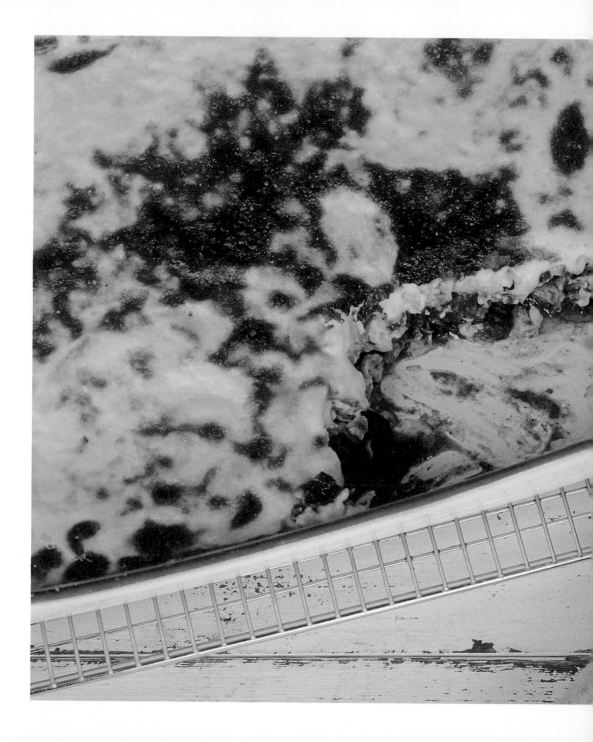

well they fit together. Spread the béchamel sauce evenly top, then sprinkle with the remaining ¼ cup Parmesan cheese. Bake for 25–30 minutes, until it's heated through, the cheese is bubbling, and the sauce is golden on top. Remove from the oven and let stand for 10 minutes before serving.

The moussaka can be stored in an airtight container in the fridge for up to 3 days. It can be easily reheated in the oven at 350°F for 15 minutes covered, then for 5 minutes uncovered. If you want an extra-bubbly top, set it under the broiler for 2–3 minutes after it comes out the oven, until sizzling again. Alternatively, you can always pop a piece in the microwave for a few minutes to reheat for a quick lunch at work.

LAMB SLIDERS with PICKLED ONION SLAW

Tiny hamburgers are so cute. And I do love the name "sliders"—it's so much more hip than "tiny burger." Have two or three of these to make a meal, or serve them as appetizers. The feta and Black Cherry dark balsamic vinegar give the lamb a lovely finish, and the toasty garlicky bread crumbs add great texture and flavor to the final dish!

———————

To prepare the slaw, place the cabbage in a heatproof bowl.

In a saucepan over medium-high heat, place the onions, white wine vinegar, and balsamic. Bring to a boil, then add the water, brown sugar, and remaining slaw ingredients. Turn down the heat to medium-low and stir to allow the onions to soften slightly and the sugar and salt to dissolve. Once the sugar and salt have dissolved, simmer for 5 minutes, allowing the spices to infuse, then remove from the heat and pour over the cabbage. Let sit, uncovered, for at least 1 hour before serving. This will keep in an airtight container in the fridge for up to 1 month.

For the sliders, heat the olive oil in a frying pan over medium heat. Add the bread crumbs and mix well so that they're fully coated in the olive oil. Toast for 2–3 minutes, until golden, then remove from the heat. Transfer the bread crumbs to a bowl and add the remaining slider ingredients. Mix well with your hands until it's a soft, creamy texture. Divide the mixture into 12, roll each piece into a ball, and flatten slightly to form small patties about 1 inch thick.

Heat your grill or a large frying pan over medium-high heat. Grill or fry the sliders for 4–5 minutes per side, until crisp and browned on the outside and cooked through. If your pan isn't nonstick, you might need a little oil for this.

Makes 12 sliders

Slaw
1 cup grated red cabbage
1 red onion, sliced into rings
½ cup white wine vinegar
¼ cup Apricot white balsamic vinegar
½ cup water
2 Tbsp brown sugar
1 cinnamon stick
1 Tbsp yellow mustard seeds
1 tsp white peppercorns
1 tsp celery seed
1 tsp sea salt

Sliders
2 Tbsp Garlic infused olive oil
1 cup dried bread crumbs
1 lb ground pork
½ lb ground lamb
2 eggs
¾ cup crumbled feta cheese
3 Tbsp chopped fresh mint leaves
2 Tbsp Black Cherry dark balsamic vinegar
1 tsp grated orange zest

To assemble
1 cup plain Greek yogurt (store-bought or homemade, see page 17)
2 Tbsp chopped fresh mint leaves
6 butter lettuce leaves
12 slider buns

While the patties are cooking, whisk together the yogurt and mint. Tear each of the lettuce leaves in half and toast the buns, if desired. Leftover yogurt will keep in an airtight container in the fridge for up to 1 week. Try using it to whip up some tzatziki (page 13)!

To assemble, spread a little mint yogurt on each side of the bun. Place the lettuce on the bottom bun, top with a patty, a few tablespoons of slaw (knocking off any extra peppercorns as you pull the slaw out of its container), and top bun. Enjoy immediately while fresh and warm.

Leftover cooked patties can be stored in an airtight container in the fridge for up to 3 days. The meat can be made in advance and kept, uncooked, in the fridge overnight or frozen for up to 3 months if desired.

You can make these into six large patties for traditional burgers or eighteen little meatballs, if desired. Cook large patties for 5–7 minutes per side; cook meatballs in a 375°F oven for 20 minutes.

Beef or chicken also works well in place of the lamb, as well as using all pork.

ROASTED LEG of LAMB

This often lands on our table for Saturday-night feasts with friends, not just on holiday occasions. Lamb cooked with the right seasoning is lovely, and I often prefer it to a beef or pork roast.

Preheat the oven to 450°F.

Pat dry the leg of lamb with paper towel.

Separate all the cloves of garlic from their skin. Using a paring knife, carefully slice small openings in the meat and insert a clove of garlic into each hole. Push the clove as far in as you can—if they're too close to the surface, they might pop out during cooking. Place the lamb on a baking tray, drizzle with 2 Tbsp of the olive oil, and sprinkle with the sea salt and paprika.

Roast in the oven for 10 minutes, until seared and crisp on the outside. Turn the leg over, and roast for another 10 minutes. Remove the lamb from the oven and turn down the heat to 325°F.

While the leg is roasting, slice the onion into rounds. Whisk together the remaining ingredients, including the remaining 2 Tbsp olive oil, for your marinade.

In a roasting pan that fits the leg of lamb snugly, place the onions in an even layer over the bottom of the pan and put the leg of lamb on top. Pour the marinade over the leg, ensuring some of the herbs and zest stay on top of the meat. Sprinkle with a little sea salt and cover with a lid or foil, making a tent if you're using foil.

Roast for 1½ hours, then baste the leg, turn it over, and roast for an additional 45 minutes. Remove the lid or foil, baste the lamb again, and roast, uncovered, for 30 minutes. The meat will pull away from the bone and will be a rich caramel brown color. Remove from the oven and allow to sit for 15 minutes before carving.

SERVES

SIX

3-4 lb bone-in leg of lamb

1 head of garlic

4 Tbsp Lemon fused olive oil, divided

2 tsp sea salt, plus extra for sprinkling

1 tsp smoked paprika

1 large yellow onion

1 cup dry white wine

¼ cup Apricot white balsamic vinegar

¼ cup grainy Dijon mustard

2 Tbsp chopped fresh rosemary leaves

1 Tbsp chopped fresh oregano leaves

2 tsp fresh thyme leaves

2 tsp grated lemon zest

For a delicious, refreshing gravy, whisk ¼ cup of pan drippings with 2 cups of plain Greek yogurt (page 17) and 2 Tbsp of chopped fresh mint leaves in a saucepan over medium heat. Add more drippings until it's the consistency of a thick gravy and serve.

LAMB LOLLIPOPS with
BLACK CHERRY GASTRIQUE

For true lamb lovers, these lollipops really could be a meal in themselves. It's quite a primal dish in that you're eating meat straight off the bone, but these are so tender, not to mention bite-size, that they're as elegant as they are caveman-like. If you don't use all the yummy cherry gastrique, try spooning it over ice cream, whisking it into barbecue sauce, or enjoying it on its own. The Lemon fused olive oil and Apricot white balsamic vinegar in the marinade create a sweetness in the meat without overpowering it so the meat shines through.

———————

To prepare the lamb, pat dry the chops with paper towel. Place them on a parchment-lined baking pan or in a roasting pan. Season with salt and pepper.

In a small bowl, whisk together the olive oil, the Apricot balsamic, and fresh ginger. Rub the mixture into both sides of the lamb chops, cover with plastic wrap, and transfer to the fridge to marinate for at least 1 hour, or up to overnight.

You can make the gastrique up to 3 weeks ahead of time and store it in the fridge in an airtight container. In a small saucepan over medium heat, place the cherries, brown sugar, wine, and Black Cherry balsamic. Bring to a low boil, then turn down the heat to medium-low, stirring occasionally to prevent sticking and gently mashing the cherries to extract any extra juices. Simmer for 20 minutes, until the sauce has reduced by half. Remove from the heat and allow to cool to room temperature. Place the cooled sauce in a blender and blend for 2–3 minutes, until you have a smooth, thin, lump-free sauce. The gastrique should easily coat the back of a spoon. If it's too watery, place it back in the saucepan and simmer for an additional 10 minutes, stirring occasionally.

SERVES
TWO-FOUR
———

Lamb Lollipops
10-12 lamb rib chops, frenched

¼ cup plus 2 Tbsp Lemon fused olive oil, divided

2 Tbsp Apricot white balsamic vinegar

2 tsp freshly grated ginger

Sea salt and cracked black pepper

2 tsp ground sumac

1 tsp ground ginger

1 Tbsp chopped fresh thyme leaves

Gastrique
2 cups fresh pitted cherries, or frozen and thawed

¾ cup brown sugar, packed

½ cup dry red wine

½ cup Black Cherry dark balsamic vinegar

Heat a frying pan over medium-high heat and drizzle in the remaining 2 Tbsp olive oil. In a small bowl, stir together the sumac and ground ginger and set aside. Remove the lamb chops from the marinade, shaking off any excess, and sprinkle each side with a little of the sumac-ginger mixture. Fry the chops for 2 minutes per side, browning the meat and searing in the juices. Do this in batches so you don't overcrowd the pan. Sprinkle the freshly cooked chops with the thyme leaves and let them rest for 5 minutes before serving. Serve with a drizzle of black cherry gastrique. Pour the remaining gastrique into a small dish so guests can add more if they like.

PASTITSIO

This Greek baked pasta is a supremely indulgent winter comfort food. The warmly spiced meat sauce, tangy feta, and creamy béchamel sauce create a unique set of flavors that meld together so well it's rather unbelievable. The Black Cherry dark balsamic vinegar in the sauce adds yet another layer of complexity. Don't be tempted to skip tossing the noodles with whisked eggs—that's what helps the pasta to hold together and not fall apart when being served.

———

Preheat the oven to 375°F. Drizzle a little olive oil into a 9- x 13-inch baking pan and spread it around to evenly coat.

In a frying pan over medium-high heat, heat the olive oil and then sauté the onions for about 2 minutes, until just translucent. Sprinkle in the salt to allow the onions to sweat for 1–2 minutes, then add the ground beef and sauté for 4–5 more minutes, until the meat is browned and the onions are soft.

Stir in the tomato paste and herbs and spices, mixing well to combine. Add the wine and balsamic. Stirring constantly for 5–10 minutes, allow the mixture to boil down and thicken. When most of the liquid has cooked down, add the tomato juice from the can, then gently crush the tomatoes with your hand before adding them to the sauce as well. Stir to combine and then add the sugar and cook down, stirring constantly, for about 5 minutes, until thick. Remove from the heat.

In a saucepan of boiling water, cook the pasta to just al dente and then drain. It should still have a bit of crunch to it, as you'll be baking it as well, so you don't want to cook it fully at this point.

While the pasta is cooking, prepare the béchamel. First, heat the olive oil in a nonstick saucepan (you need

SERVES
SIX-EIGHT

———

Meat Sauce

2 Tbsp Garlic infused olive oil

1 medium yellow onion, cut in ¼-inch dice

1 tsp sea salt

1 lb ground beef

2 Tbsp tomato paste

2 bay leaves

1 tsp finely chopped fresh oregano leaves

1 tsp finely chopped fresh curly-leaf parsley

1 tsp ground cinnamon

½ tsp ground cloves

½ tsp freshly grated or ground nutmeg

¾ cup dry red wine

¼ cup Black Cherry dark balsamic vinegar

1 (28 oz) can whole plum tomatoes

2 tsp granulated sugar

Béchamel Sauce

¼ cup Garlic infused olive oil

¼ cup all-purpose flour

1 cup 2% milk

1 cup heavy (35%) cream

2 egg yolks

nonstick for this recipe) over medium heat. Whisk in the flour. It will bubble up and foam, then reduce down to a creamy paste. Add 3–4 Tbsp of the milk, stirring continuously. Still stirring, slowly add the remaining milk and then the cream. Once all of the cream has been added, remove the pan from the heat. Whisk in the egg yolks, nutmeg, and salt to taste. When the mixture is fully combined, add ¾ cup of the Parmesan cheese.

In a large bowl, whisk together the eggs, egg whites, and olive oil. Add the hot pasta. Toss to combine, ensuring the pasta is well coated in the egg mixture, and transfer to the prepared baking pan. Spread the feta evenly across the pasta. Pour the meat sauce over the top, spreading it in an even layer and mixing it slightly with the pasta to ensure all is well coated. Spread the béchamel sauce over the meat sauce and finish with the remaining ¼ cup Parmesan cheese.

Bake for 25 minutes, until the top is bubbling and golden brown. Remove from the oven and immediately run a knife around the outside of the pan. Let it sit for 5 minutes before serving.

Leftovers can be stored in an airtight container in the fridge for up to 3 days.

¼ tsp freshly grated
or ground nutmeg

1 tsp sea salt

1 cup freshly grated Parmesan
cheese, divided

Pasta

1 lb penne pasta

2 eggs + 2 egg whites

2 Tbsp Garlic Infused olive oil

½ cup crumbled feta cheese

BEEF STEW with ROASTED BELL PEPPERS

This hearty stew is so simple, and yet so flavorful. While I often serve it for holidays or Sunday meals, it's also one of our weeknight favorites. If I'm in a rush, I'll brown the meat and add all the ingredients to the slow cooker. As soon as I open the door in the evening, I'm greeted with a sweet, intense aroma.

Line a plate with paper towel.

In a shallow bowl, place the flour and sprinkle it with salt and pepper to taste. Pat dry the beef with paper towel and dredge it through the flour mixture, shaking off any excess.

In a large frying pan or Dutch oven over medium-high heat, heat the olive oil and then add the beef, a few pieces at a time to avoid overcrowding the pan, and brown it on all sides. Transfer it to the prepared plate.

Add the onions and whole cloves of garlic to the pan. Turn down the heat to medium-low and sauté for 2–3 minutes. Sprinkle with 1 tsp of the black pepper and the 1 tsp sea salt to help the onions sweat, and sauté for 3–5 minutes, until the onions are browned and soft. Remove from the heat.

If you're using a slow cooker, place the onions in the slow cooker.

If you're using the oven, preheat it to 350°F. Place the onions in a casserole dish large enough to hold everything without overcrowding.

Whichever method you're using, slice the roasted bell peppers into 1-inch-wide strips and add a few of them to the onions. Place the meat on top of the peppers, top the meat with the remaining peppers, pour the stewed tomatoes and balsamic over the top, and sprinkle with the remaining 1 tsp black pepper.

SERVES
FOUR

½ cup all-purpose flour

Sea salt and cracked black pepper

¼ cup Garlic infused olive oil

2 lb stewing beef

2 large yellow onions, roughly chopped

8 garlic cloves

2 tsp cracked black pepper, divided

1 tsp sea salt

8 large roasted red, orange, or yellow (or a mix) bell peppers (see sidebar on the next page)

1 (14 oz) can stewed tomatoes

¼ cup Black Cherry dark balsamic vinegar

1 cup fresh mint leaves

If you're using a slow cooker, cook on low for 6–8 hours.

If you're using the oven, cover the casserole dish and bake for 2–2½ hours, until the meat is tender and the sauce is very thick. Check on it after the first hour. If the stew is drying out, add 2–3 Tbsp of water or stock to prevent burning.

Gently stir in the mint before serving. Serve this with crusty bread, or for a more special occasion, Lemon Roasted Potatoes (page 117) and Fresh Greek Salad (page 55).

Leftovers will keep in an airtight container in the fridge for up to 1 week. The flavors will continue to develop, so this is an ideal leftovers dish.

To roast your own peppers, sear the peppers over a grill or under the broiler until the skin is black and peeling away from the outside of the pepper on all sides. Use tongs to do this and don't rush. Take your time and ensure they're well charred. I turn my peppers a quarter turn every 3–4 minutes and continue to rotate as they roast. Allow the peppers to cool completely. Peel back the skin, slice the peppers in half, and remove the seeds and membrane. Brush the flesh with a little Garlic infused olive oil and store in an airtight container in the fridge for up to 1 week.

GREEK-STYLE PORK RIBS

Slow and low is always my mantra when it comes to ribs. I've given the honey garlic glaze a Greek twist here, so these are ideal for a summer grill, or for a winter meal when you're dreaming of summer, or even cold for a picnic. The tangy lemon juice adds a fresh zesty flavor, the Garlic infused olive oil adds a savoriness, and the Black Cherry dark balsamic vinegar rounds it all out and ensures the outside is nice and caramelized.

Line a baking pan with parchment paper.

In a small bowl, whisk together the olive oil, honey, balsamic, lemon juice and zest, herbs, paprika, and salt and pepper.

Place the ribs meat side down on the prepared baking pan, separated by at least 2 inches. You might need two baking pans and two racks in the oven. If this is the case, rotate the pans top to bottom when you first baste the ribs about halfway through roasting to ensure even cooking.

Pour half the marinade over the ribs, then turn them over and pour the remaining marinade over them. Allow to sit in the fridge, uncovered, for 2–3 hours, or overnight, to marinate.

Preheat the oven to 375°F.

Bake the ribs, uncovered, for 5 minutes. Turn them over and bake for an additional 5 minutes. Then, without opening the oven door, turn down the heat to 275°F and allow the ribs to keep cooking for 1½ hours. (You don't need to wait for the oven to reach 275°F before you start timing this part.)

Baste the ribs in the marinade juices at the bottom of the pan, flip them over, and baste again with the marinade. Bake for another 30 minutes, then repeat the process

¼ cup Garlic infused olive oil

¼ cup honey

¼ cup Black Cherry dark
balsamic vinegar

Juice and zest from 1 lemon

2 Tbsp chopped fresh
rosemary leaves

2 Tbsp chopped fresh
oregano leaves

1 Tbsp smoked paprika

2 tsp sea salt

2 tsp cracked black pepper

2 racks of pork ribs
(back or side ribs,
3-4 lb in total)

(baste, flip, baste) and bake for an additional 30 minutes. The meat will be pulling away from the bone and the ribs may have fallen apart during the flipping process. This means they're tender and delicious!

At this point, I recommend you switch to using your grill. Preheat it to high heat. Otherwise, take the ribs out of the oven and increase the oven temperature to 400°F.

Place the ribs directly on the grill, or place the baking pan back in the hot oven, and baste with the marinade drippings. Flip after 5–7 minutes, or once the ribs are nicely caramelized and crisp on the outside. Baste them again, and cook for 3–5 minutes, until caramelized and crisp. Serve immediately with lots of tzatziki (page 13) for dipping. These are lovely with Tomato and Kalamata Flatbread (page 23) and the Fresh Leek and Olive Salad (page 57) for a simple and extra-tasty meal.

If there happen to be any leftover ribs (highly unlikely), they can be stored in an airtight container in the fridge for up to 3 days.

SAUSAGE-STUFFED BRAISED CABBAGE LEAVES

Not quite cabbage rolls, this winter dish is rustic and delicious from beginning to end. Traditionally served with béchamel or avgolemono sauce, these little sausage bundles are a delicious addition to a vegetable-based meal for those who can't do without their meat. The balsamic tenderizes the meat and adds a unique sweetness to the pork, which reveals a lovely, complex flavor that you wouldn't get from dried apricots.

———————————

Line a plate with paper towel.

Bring a large saucepan of water to a boil and then remove it from the heat. Immerse the head of cabbage in the hot water. If you don't think you'll use the entire head of cabbage, carefully peel off some leaves and blanch them. (I find that the leaves usually break, though, so I usually end up blanching the head whole and peeling the leaves off afterward.)

Using sharp kitchen scissors, cut out the spine of each leaf and lay the leaves on the prepared plate.

In a large bowl, mix together the pork, egg whites, feta, dill, balsamic, and lemon zest until the mixture is smooth and fully incorporated.

Using your hands, pinch off 1–1½ Tbsp of the mixture, roll it into a ball, then squish it gently into an oval-shaped meatball.

Place each meatball at the top of the cabbage leaf. Fold the tails of the cabbage leaf up around the sausage, then fold in the sides and roll the leaf the rest of the way up, so the sausage is entirely encased in the cabbage leaf, burrito-style.

Place the roll on a baking tray and repeat with the remaining sausage meat.

SERVES
FOUR
———

1 small green cabbage

1 lb ground pork

2 eggs, separated

¾ cup crumbled feta cheese, plus extra for garnish

¼ cup chopped fresh dill, plus extra for garnish

2 Tbsp Apricot white balsamic vinegar

Juice and zest from 1 lemon

2 Tbsp ouzo

If you're freezing these for later, place the baking tray in the freezer for 6–8 hours and then transfer the leaves to resealable plastic bags and freeze for up to 3 months.

When you're ready to cook and serve, preheat the oven to 350°F. Place the sausage-stuffed cabbage packets in an even layer in a baking dish just large enough to hold them snugly. Add 1–2 cups of water to cover the sausage three-quarters of the way up, then drizzle with the ouzo, and bake, covered, for 35–40 minutes if cooking from fresh, and 1 hour if cooking from frozen.

Meanwhile, in a bowl set over a pot of simmering water, whisk together the two egg yolks and lemon juice until the mixture is thick enough to coat the back of a spoon.

To serve, remove the cabbage leaves from the baking dish. Arrange them on a serving plate, drizzle with sauce, and sprinkle with feta and dill for garnish, and serve with more sauce on the side.

ROASTED CHICKEN SOUVLAKI

This classic recipe is traditionally cooked on the grill and served kebab-style, as shown in the accompanying photo, but I also make it by roasting chicken legs or breasts in the oven when the grill isn't handy—or it's buried under snow. Lovely with tzatziki (page 13), pita (page 19), and all the fixings on the side, or made into a salad of sorts, this recipe is made for playing with. The marinade is the secret ingredient. I often freeze the meat in the marinade so I can pull it off for a quick weeknight meal (that's my idea of fast food!).

SERVES
FOUR

4 large chicken breasts, skin on, bone in

¼ cup Lemon fused olive oil

¼ cup Garlic infused olive oil

2 Tbsp grainy Dijon mustard

2 Tbsp Apricot white balsamic vinegar

1 Tbsp chopped fresh curly-leaf parsley

2 tsp chopped fresh oregano leaves

1 tsp grated lemon zest

Pinch of ground chili (Aleppo is my favorite, although cayenne is lovely too.)

Sea salt and cracked black pepper

Place the chicken breasts in a plastic bag or baking dish large enough to hold them snugly without overcrowding.

Whisk together the remaining ingredients, and pour the resulting marinade over the chicken. Lift the skin of the chicken slightly so the marinade can get under it to the meat. You might need to rub it into the skin so it's evenly distributed under and on the skin. If you're using a baking dish, cover it tightly. Allow to marinate for 2–3 hours in the fridge, or overnight.

Preheat the grill—or, if using the oven, preheat it to 400°F.

If cooking directly on the grill, cook 4–5 minutes per side.

If cooking in the oven, arrange the chicken on a baking tray and drizzle with the residual marinade. Sprinkle with salt and pepper.

Bake, uncovered, for 25–30 minutes, until the skin is golden and crispy and the juices run clear when the chicken is pierced. Serve with Lemon Roasted Potatoes (page 117), Fresh Greek Salad (page 55), pita (page 19), and tzatziki (page 13).

Leftover chicken can be stored in an airtight container in the fridge for up to 3 days.

To make kebab-style, follow the recipe but cube and skewer the 4 boneless chicken breasts. Grill or bake as directed here, baking in the oven for 15 to 20 minutes, or grilling for less than that on a hot, outdoor grill.

CHICKEN and APRICOT PIE

This is one of the few recipes where I like using phyllo pastry, because if it breaks, it makes the final product more rustic and beautiful. A Greek take on a meat pie, this dish is lovely hot or served chilled the next day. Its warm spices make it perfect for a winter weeknight meal.

———————————

Rinse the barley well and place it in a heavy-bottomed saucepan over medium-high heat. Finely chop the apricots and add them to the barley, along with the cloves. Pour in the stock, cover, and bring to a rolling boil. Turn down the heat to low and simmer, covered, for 35–40 minutes, until the barley is tender but still meaty in texture. Remove the whole cloves.

Meanwhile, chop the onion and sauté it in 2 Tbsp of the olive oil in a frying pan over medium heat for 5–10 minutes, until just translucent. Sprinkle in the salt, cinnamon, and allspice, then add the ground chicken and continue to sauté, using a wooden spoon to break up the chicken into a fine mince, for 3–5 minutes, until the chicken is fully browned and the onions are starting to darken. Remove from the heat and add the barley mixture to the chicken, mixing well to combine. Mix in the yogurt, balsamic, herbs, and pepper, mixing well.

Preheat the oven to 375°F. Brush the bottom and sides of a 10-inch pie plate with some of the remaining olive oil.

Gently brush the top of four of the phyllo sheets with olive oil and arrange them, oiled side up, in the pie plate, allowing the corners to drape over the edge. Rotate each sheet slightly so that the corners aren't overlapping. You want a pointy pattern around the outside of the dish. If some of the sheets rip or break, that's totally OK.

Place the filling on top of the phyllo. Brush another four sheets with olive oil and drape them over the top of the pie,

SERVES
SIX
———

1 cup dried pearl barley

8-10 dried apricots

6 whole cloves

3 cups chicken stock

1 small yellow onion

4 Tbsp Lemon fused olive oil

1 tsp sea salt, plus extra for sprinkling

½ tsp ground cinnamon

½ tsp ground allspice

1 lb ground chicken

½ cup plain Greek yogurt (store-bought or homemade, see page 17)

2 Tbsp Apricot white balsamic vinegar

1 Tbsp chopped fresh oregano leaves

1 tsp chopped fresh rosemary leaves

½ tsp cracked black pepper

10 sheets phyllo pastry

again rotating them so that the corners don't overlap and letting them drape over the edge of the dish. Gently fold in the overhanging phyllo to create a rolled look around the outside. Again, if it breaks, that's totally OK.

Brush the remaining two sheets of phyllo with oil and crumple them up together in a ball. Place them on the top of the pie, flattened slightly, so you have a bumpy, creased top (trust me, it will be beautiful when finished!). Brush the top of the pie with a little more olive oil and sprinkle with some sea salt.

Bake for 25–30 minutes, until heated through and the pastry is puffed and golden. Remove from the oven and let sit for 10 minutes before serving.

This is best eaten the day you make it, as it doesn't reheat very well. It's excellent when enjoyed cold the next day and will keep in the fridge in an airtight container for up to 4 days.

ROASTED CHICKEN with DRIED FRUIT

There's something really special about roasting meat with fruit. The fruit keeps the meat sweet and juicy and adds a unique complexity to the overall flavor of this dish.

SERVES
FOUR

1 (5-6 lb) roasting chicken

1 red onion

1 lemon

2 heads of garlic

2 sprigs of rosemary

2 cups assorted dried fruit
(dates, prunes, apricots, etc.)

4 Tbsp extra virgin olive oil

Sea salt and cracked black pepper

½ cup Apricot white
balsamic vinegar

½ cup dry white wine

Pat dry the chicken with paper towel and place it in a large roasting pan, leaving at least 2–3 inches of space around the chicken. Preheat the oven to 400°F.

Slice the onion and lemon into four to six wedges each, and slice the top off the heads of garlic, keeping the skin on and the cloves intact. Place two onion wedges and two lemon wedges inside the cavity of the chicken. Arrange the remaining wedges around the outside of the bird and the heads of garlic in opposite corners. Tuck the sprigs of rosemary along each side of the bird, but not tucked underneath.

Scatter the dried fruit around the chicken, tucking a few pieces in the cavity and under the wings and legs.

Drizzle the chicken with 2 Tbsp of the olive oil and rub it all over, then drizzle the remaining 2 Tbsp of olive oil over the heads of garlic, making sure that it all seeps in. Season the chicken with salt and pepper, then pour the balsamic and wine into the pan around but not over the chicken.

Roast, uncovered, in the oven for 50–55 minutes, until the internal temperature reaches 165°F and the skin is golden brown.

Remove from the oven, and let rest for 5 minutes before carving and serving. Scoop some of the fruit out from the drippings and spoon it over the meat before serving. If the mood strikes you, tuck in some fresh plums and apricots into the baking dish as soon as the chicken comes out of the oven to add color and flavor to the dish.

Leftovers will keep in an airtight container in the fridge for up to 3 days.

Try serving this with Lemon Roasted Potatoes (page 117), Cretan Roasted Beet Salad (page 59), or Braised Stuffed Peppers and Tomatoes (page 112).

SEAFOOD PILAF

Warm and refreshing, this rice dish is superflexible when it comes to the seafood. It's a great way to use up extras from the freezer, but also an excuse to buy an assortment of shellfish. A mix of prawns, mussels, and white fish is my favorite. The rice is toasted first, which gives an extra nuttiness to the final dish.

Rinse the seafood and pat dry with paper towel. If you're using clams or mussels, trim off the beards and scrub the shells.

Heat the Garlic infused olive oil in a heavy-bottomed frying pan or Dutch oven over medium heat, and fry the seafood (minus any clams or mussels) in batches, being careful not to crowd the pan, for 1–2 minutes to sear the outside. Remove from the pan and set aside.

Finely chop the onion and sauté for 1–2 minutes. Add the sea salt to allow the onions to sweat for 2–3 minutes. When they're just starting to brown, add the rice and mix well to coat it in the olive oil. Cook for 2–3 minutes more, until the rice is translucent. Add the lemon juice, zest, and balsamic, and stir until the liquid has been fully absorbed.

Pour in the stock and cover the pan. Turn down the heat as low as possible and simmer for 25–30 minutes, until almost all the liquid has been absorbed and the rice is tender yet still stiff in texture. Fluff the rice with a fork and mix in the fresh herbs and any shellfish. Cover and simmer for 5 minutes, then fluff again and add the seared seafood and the Lemon fused olive oil. Cook, stirring gently, for 2–3 minutes, adding a little water or stock if necessary.

This dish doesn't keep well, so try to eat it the day you make it. If leftovers are stored, keep them in an airtight container in the fridge and enjoy them the next day.

SERVES
FOUR

---

1 lb mixed seafood (a mix of shellfish and scaled, boneless white fish is perfect)

¼ cup Garlic infused olive oil

1 red onion

1 tsp sea salt

1½ cups uncooked long-grain rice

Juice and zest of 1 lemon

2 Tbsp Apricot white balsamic vinegar

3 cups fish stock, or a mild vegetable stock

2 Tbsp chopped fresh dill, plus extra for garnish

2 tsp chopped fresh curly-leaf parsley

2 Tbsp Lemon fused olive oil

Lemon wedges for garnish

Not a seafood lover? Substitute the same amount of chicken instead!

OVEN-BAKED COD

Fennel works really well with fish. Its aniseed flavor is subtle and yet unmistakably present. It's a great alternative to dill. The Lemon fused olive oil makes this dish supremely moist and flavorful.

SERVES
FOUR

2 fennel bulbs
4 Tbsp Lemon fused olive oil
2 Tbsp fennel seeds
3 garlic cloves
1 tsp sea salt
½ tsp cracked black pepper
2 Tbsp grainy Dijon mustard
1 (3-4 lb) piece of cod

———————

Preheat the broiler.

Trim the top, bottom, and outer layers of the fennel and slice the bulbs into ½-inch-thick slices. Arrange the slices evenly in a roasting pan. Drizzle with 2 Tbsp of the olive oil and place under the broiler for 4–5 minutes, until the fennel is starting to brown and blister slightly.

Preheat the oven to 350°F.

Gently toast the fennel seeds in a small frying pan over low heat for 2–3 minutes, until their aroma is potent and they're starting to turn golden brown.

Pour the seeds into a mortar and pestle and coarsely grind them while they're still warm. Add the remaining 2 Tbsp of olive oil, garlic, and salt and pepper, and continue to grind and mash to form a chunky paste. Add the mustard and mix well.

Wash and pat dry the fish, and place it on top of the blistered fennel. Spread the fennel seed mixture over the fish, coating it well.

Bake, covered, for 20 minutes, until the fish is cooked through and the fennel is well roasted and tender. Serve immediately.

Leftovers will keep in an airtight container in the fridge for up to 2 days.

Seabass, halibut, and salmon are also great options for this dish.

SOUFICO (SMOTHERED VEGETABLE STEW)

The variations and options for this hearty vegetable main are really endless. You can mix and match the vegetables to your heart's content. The end result is an incredibly delicious cross between scalloped potatoes and ratatouille. Using a mix of Lemon fused olive oil and extra virgin olive oil ensures the lemon doesn't overpower any other ingredient, but instead adds a lovely freshness to the dish, whatever the time of year.

Lightly grease a 9- × 9-inch baking pan with some extra virgin olive oil. Line a baking tray with paper towel.

Slice the zucchini and eggplant into ¼-inch-thick rounds. Cut the tops off the peppers, discard the seeds, and slice the peppers into ¼-inch-thick rounds. Lay out all the vegetable slices in a single layer on the prepared baking tray, sprinkle with the salt, and top with another layer of paper towel. Let sit for 30 minutes to 1 hour to drain off the extra water.

Roughly chop the onion and crush the garlic cloves. In a heavy-bottomed frying pan over medium heat, heat 2 Tbsp of the Lemon fused olive oil. Add the onions and garlic, and sauté for 5–6 minutes, until the onions are softened and caramelized. Remove from the heat. Place the onions and garlic in the prepared baking pan. Sprinkle with one-quarter of the fresh herbs.

Peel the sweet potato and slice it into ¼-inch-thick rounds. Add the remaining 2 Tbsp Lemon fused olive oil to the frying pan (there's no need to wipe it clean first), and fry the sweet potatoes, in batches, for 2–3 minutes per side, until the edges are just starting to brown.

Arrange the sweet potatoes evenly on top of the onions and sprinkle one-third of the remaining fresh herbs over the top.

SERVES
FOUR

2 zucchini, skin on, scrubbed

1 large eggplant, skin on, scrubbed

3 red bell peppers

2 tsp sea salt

1 large red onion

4 garlic cloves

4 Tbsp Lemon fused olive oil

2 Tbsp chopped fresh mint leaves

1 Tbsp chopped fresh oregano leaves

1 tsp chopped fresh rosemary leaves

1 large or 2 small sweet potatoes

¼ cup extra virgin olive oil

Sea salt and cracked black pepper

Minted yogurt (page 17) or crumbled feta cheese, to serve

Preheat the oven to 350°F.

In the frying pan, fry the zucchini for 1–2 minutes per side, until golden brown and crisp, then do the same for the eggplant, and add them to the baking dish, tucking the zucchini pieces in between the eggplant pieces, and sprinkle with the remaining herbs. Top the dish with the slices of peppers, generously drizzle the extra virgin olive oil over the top, and sprinkle with salt and pepper to taste.

Bake the vegetables, uncovered, for 35–40 minutes, until they are all soft and have almost melted together. Remove from the oven and serve immediately with a dollop of minted yogurt or topped with crumbled feta.

You can store any leftovers in an airtight container in the fridge for up to 3 days.

PUMPKIN YAM MOUSSAKA

Greeks do love their moussaka, and this lovely veggie version has become a fall favorite in our home. The feta-packed cheesy béchamel sauce pairs perfectly with the root vegetables. Yams and pumpkins are a huge part of Greek cuisine and are often used in both sweet and savory dishes, so putting them in this classic Greek dish was an easy and delicious decision. The Apricot white balsamic vinegar adds a unique quality to the dish, and really brings out the caramel sweetness of the pumpkin and yam. This could almost be dessert!

————————————

Line a plate with paper towel.

Peel and seed the pumpkin, then slice it into ¼-inch-thick slices. I typically use a mandoline for this to make the process faster.

Peel the yams and slice them into ¼-inch-thick rounds. Slice the zucchini into ¼-inch slices as well.

Place the zucchini on the prepared plate and sprinkle it with 1 tsp of the salt to drain some of the water. Cover with more paper towel and set aside for 10–15 minutes.

Roughly chop the onions and sauté them in 2 Tbsp of the oil in a frying pan over medium heat for 3–5 minutes, until soft and translucent. Sprinkle with the remaining 1 tsp sea salt, sauté for 1–2 minutes, then add 2 Tbsp of the balsamic. Sauté for an additional 2–3 minutes, scraping up any bits of onion from the pan, then add the tomatoes and herbs, and simmer for 10–15 minutes, until the sauce is thick and rich.

Preheat the oven to 350°F. Grease a 9- × 13-inch baking pan with a little extra virgin olive oil.

Spread some of the tomato sauce over the bottom to form a thin, even layer.

SERVES
SIX-EIGHT

Filling

1 small pie pumpkin (see page 53)

2 medium yams

2 large zucchini, skin on, scrubbed

2 tsp sea salt, divided

2 red onions

4 Tbsp Garlic infused olive oil, divided

4 Tbsp Apricot white balsamic vinegar, divided

1 (28 oz) can crushed tomatoes

½ cup chopped fresh mint leaves

2 Tbsp chopped fresh oregano leaves

2 Tbsp chopped fresh curly-leaf parsley

1 cup all-purpose flour

Béchamel Sauce

¼ cup Garlic infused olive oil

¼ cup all-purpose flour

1 cup 2% milk

1 cup heavy (35%) cream

2 egg yolks

Pinch of freshly grated or ground nutmeg

Sea salt

1 cup crumbled feta cheese, divided

Pat the zucchini dry with the top layer of paper towel, removing any extra water.

Place ½ cup of the flour in a shallow plate and dredge a few pumpkin slices through it, shaking off any excess.

Add the remaining 2 Tbsp olive oil to the frying pan (there's no need to wipe it out first) and sear the pumpkin for 1–2 minutes on each side, until just brown. Place an even layer of pumpkin slices over the tomato sauce. Top with a very thin layer of tomato sauce, the repeat the process with the yams, zucchini, then the pumpkin again, adding a little tomato sauce between layers. Add the remaining flour to the plate as needed. Continue until all the vegetables are layered in the pan. Drizzle the vegetables with the remaining 2 Tbsp of balsamic.

To prepare the béchamel sauce, heat the olive oil in a nonstick saucepan (you need nonstick for this recipe) over medium heat. Whisk in the flour. It will bubble up and foam, then reduce down to a creamy paste. Add 3–4 Tbsp of the milk, stirring continuously. Still stirring, slowly add the remaining milk and then the cream. Once all of the cream has been added, remove the pan from the heat. Whisk in the egg yolks, nutmeg, and salt to taste. When the mixture is fully combined, add ¾ cup of the feta cheese. Pour the béchamel over the vegetables, and top with remaining feta cheese.

Bake for 35–40 minutes, until the vegetables are tender and the béchamel is golden and bubbling around the edges. Remove from the oven, and let sit for 5–10 minutes before serving.

This can be stored in an airtight container for up to 3 days in the fridge.

If fresh pumpkin isn't available, butternut squash is a lovely substitute, or even potatoes.

BRAISED STUFFED PEPPERS and TOMATOES

There are endless variations of this dish. Some have more of a meatball stuffing, some include rice, others use bread crumbs and cheese for a veggie option—whatever the stuffing, whether braised in tomato or stock, stuffed peppers and tomatoes are divine. Use firm, well-shaped peppers and tomatoes so they don't split during the cooking process. Adding Apricot white balsamic vinegar and Black Cherry dark balsamic vinegar introduces a rich new dimension to this old staple. They also help to caramelize and flavor every aspect of this dish.

_____

Preheat the oven to 350°F.

Place the raisins in a small bowl, pour boiling water over them, and set aside.

Carefully slice the tops off the tomatoes and the peppers and place back the tops so you don't mix them up. Gently cut out, or use a spoon (a grapefruit spoon with the pointy tip is great for this) to scoop out, the seeds and pulp from the tomatoes and set aside. Carefully cut out the membrane of the pepper and remove all the seeds.

Trim off the top of the fennel. Chop the dill-like fronds and set aside ¼ cup. Trim the bottom and outer layers of the fennel and dice the bulbs. Heat 2 Tbsp of the olive oil in a frying pan over medium-high heat, and fry the onions for 2–3 minutes, until just translucent. Add the chopped fennel bulb, sprinkle with salt and pepper to taste, and sauté for another 2–3 minutes. Add the ground beef, breaking it up with your wooden spoon, and Black Cherry balsamic and sauté for 3–5 minutes, until it's just brown.

Drain the liquid from the can of tomatoes into a measuring cup. Add the tomatoes to the frying pan, either squishing with your hands before dropping them in, or breaking them up with your spoon as the filling continues

SERVES
FOUR
_____

1 cup golden raisins

4 large on-the-vine tomatoes

4 large bell peppers, any color although a variety is beautiful

4 Tbsp Garlic infused olive oil, divided

1 red onion, diced

1 fennel bulb

Sea salt and cracked black pepper

½ lb ground beef

2 Tbsp Black Cherry dark balsamic vinegar

1 (28 oz) can whole plum tomatoes

½ cup uncooked short-grain rice

¼ cup fresh mint leaves

¼ cup fresh curly-leaf parsley leaves

¼ cup fresh wild fennel (top of the bulb used above)

1 cup crumbled feta cheese

½ cup dry white wine or Apricot white balsamic vinegar, or a mixture of the two to cook. Drain the raisins. Add the raisins, rice, reserved fennel fronds, and herbs, bring to a boil, then turn down the heat to low and simmer for about 10 minutes, until the rice is just tender. Remove from the heat and allow to cool slightly in the pan. Any remaining juices will be absorbed by the rice. Mix in the crumbled feta. The sauce should be thick with no large pieces of meat or vegetables.

Carefully arrange the tomatoes and peppers in a baking dish big enough to hold them snugly without crowding. Gently stuff the peppers and tomatoes three-quarters full. Do not overfill them or they'll burst. Place the tops on each tomato and pepper and drizzle with the remaining 2 Tbsp olive oil.

Pour the reserved tomato juice and wine or Apricot balsamic into the base of the baking dish around the vegetables. Sprinkle with salt and pepper to taste.

Bake for 45–50 minutes, until the tomatoes and peppers are tender and the centers are very hot.

Serve fresh from the oven in shallow bowls. Spoon some extra juices over the top of the vegetables just before serving. These are best eaten the day you make them.

Uncooked extra peppers and tomatoes can be stored in an airtight container in the fridge for up to 2 days, or frozen for up to 2 months in the freezer. Allow to thaw completely before cooking in the sauce as directed.

LEMON ROASTED POTATOES

Potatoes are such a great comfort food—the crispy outside and soft pillow-like inside somehow just speak comfort. The bright Lemon fused olive oil and tangy Garlic infused olive oil bring them to a whole new level.

Preheat the oven to 375°F. Line a baking tray with parchment paper. Bring a large saucepan of water to a boil over high heat.

Wash and scrub the potatoes, but don't peel them, and cut them into 1-inch wedges. Place the potatoes in the boiling water and turn down the heat to medium. Cook, uncovered, for 5 minutes, until the potatoes are only just fork-tender, but not fully cooked.

Drain the potatoes, rinse them under cold water to stop the cooking process, and then place them on the prepared baking tray.

In a small bowl, whisk together both olive oils, the stock, 2 Tbsp of the lemon juice, and salt and pepper to taste. Drizzle this over the potatoes and shake to coat them evenly. Roast in the oven for 18–20 minutes, until golden brown and crispy.

Remove from the oven, and, keeping the potatoes in the pan, sprinkle them with oregano and the remaining 2 Tbsp lemon juice. Shake the pan (with oven mitts on!) to coat the potatoes in the lemon juice again. Serve immediately. Serve these alongside lamb sliders (page 71) or moussaka (page 64), or on their own for a tasty treat.

In the unlikely event of there being any leftovers, you can store them in an airtight container in the fridge for up to 1 week. (They're amazing heated up in a frying pan with some extra virgin olive oil or pan drippings the next morning for breakfast! Try a drizzle of lemon juice over the top for a zingy start to your day.)

SERVES

FOUR

---

4 large baking potatoes (russet or Yukon gold are best)

¼ cup Lemon fused olive oil

¼ cup Garlic infused olive oil

¼ cup vegetable or chicken stock

4 Tbsp lemon juice (1-2 lemons), divided

Sea salt and cracked black pepper

1 Tbsp fresh oregano leaves

The trick to these potatoes is to parboil them first, adding moisture to the inside and reducing the cooking time to finish them off, and then dousing them with lemon juice as soon as they come out of the oven.

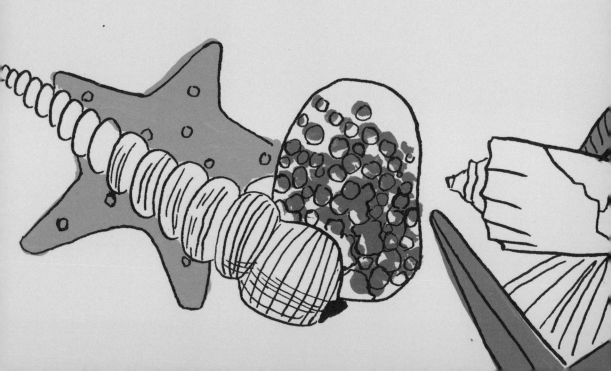

SWEETS

GRILLED PEACHES with YOGURT and HONEY

One of the simplest desserts you can make for a late summer BBQ, these grilled peaches are divine. I let the peaches get a bit charred, as I find they develop a lovely light caramel flavor that way. Allowing the vinegar to really reduce makes them extra delicious. I love to serve them with a gingersnap or the Greek Christmas cookies (page 143) (especially if I'm craving those Christmas cookies in the summer—it's a great excuse to make them for Christmas in July!).

Preheat a grill—charcoal or propane. Sadly, these aren't the best grilled in the oven or under the broiler, so don't even think about it.

In a small bowl, whisk together the Greek yogurt, honey, and 1 Tbsp of the balsamic. Set aside at room temperature until ready to serve.

Wash and dry the peaches. Leaving the skin on, cut them in half and discard the pits.

Brush the cut side of the peach halves with the olive oil and place them cut side down on the grill. Grill for 3–4 minutes, until strong grill marks are visible and the peach is almost charred and softening slightly. Flip the peaches over and drizzle the remaining balsamic over the cut surface of each half. Grill for an additional 3–4 minutes.

To serve, place each peach half on a small plate, cut side up, and top with a dollop of the Greek yogurt mixture. Serve immediately.

If you have leftovers, slice the peaches and store them in an airtight container for up to 1 week in the fridge. Store the yogurt mixture in a separate airtight container for up to 1 week in the fridge.

SERVES
FOUR

1 cup plain Greek yogurt (store-bought or homemade, see page 17)

2 Tbsp honey

2 Tbsp Apricot white balsamic vinegar, divided

2 peaches

1 Tbsp Lemon fused olive oil

STEWED CHERRIES

Cherries are one of my favorite fruit—from the stunning blossoms that let us know spring really is here to the cherry trees I climbed as a kid just to pick the delicious fruit from the tree, there are memories in every bite. Stewed cherries are still my favorite ice cream topping, and even in winter I'll find a bag of frozen cherries and make this to remind me of summer and how much I love it. The warm spices in this recipe create a delicious and addictive flavor profile, and the Cherry dark balsamic deepens the cherry flavor so much that even if your berries aren't the best, this recipe is delicious every time.

In a large saucepan over medium heat, bring the balsamic, water, sugar, and spices to a boil. Turn down the heat and simmer, uncovered, for 5 minutes. Add the cherries and continue to simmer until the cherries are soft and tender.

Remove from the heat and allow to cool completely. Spoon into an airtight container and store in the fridge for up to 1 month. When serving, spoon out the cherries and leave the spices in the jar.

Makes 4 cups

½ cup Cherry dark balsamic vinegar

⅓ cup water

⅓ cup granulated sugar

6 whole green cardamom pods

1 tsp whole white peppercorns

1 bay leaf

1 long pepper (see below)

1 whole star anise

3 cups fresh pitted or frozen sweet cherries

Long peppers taste a little like cinnamon and nutmeg and white pepper combined, and look like tiny pinecones. They're available in most spice stores.

BAKLAVA TURNOVERS

Working with phyllo pastry can be fussy, so here is this classic dessert in turnover form. Walnuts and pistachios are the most traditional nuts for baklava, sometimes in combination, but almonds, hazelnuts, and pecans are also used. Walnuts work particularly well with lemon olive oil, so that's what's used here.

Preheat the oven to 350°F. Line a baking tray with parchment paper.

On a floured surface, gently roll out each piece of puff pastry into a 12- × 12-inch square. Brush the rectangle with 2 Tbsp of Lemon fused olive oil and, using a pizza cutter or sharp knife, cut it into six rectangles. Repeat with the second square of puff pastry and set aside. (See sidebar on page 35.)

In a small saucepan over medium heat, stir together the remaining ¼ cup Lemon fused olive oil, the honey, sugar, water, spices, and salt and bring to a simmer. Allow to simmer, still over medium heat, for 7–8 minutes, to form a thick syrup. Add the nuts and mix well, ensuring that the nuts are evenly coated in the syrup.

To assemble, take one pastry square and brush the edges with a little bit of water. Scoop 2 Tbsp of the nut mixture into the center of the square. Fold two opposite corners together to form a triangle and press gently together to seal. Place on the prepared baking tray, and repeat with the remaining puff pastry squares.

In a small bowl, whisk together the egg and 2 Tbsp olive oil. Gently brush this egg wash over the pastries. Bake for 15–17 minutes, until golden brown and puffed.

Allow to sit for 5 minutes before serving. The honey nut mixture inside will be very hot and does hold its heat! These will keep in an airtight container for up to 1 week.

SERVES
FOUR-SIX

Makes 12 turnovers

1 (8 oz) package frozen puff pastry, thawed

¼ cup + 2 Tbsp Lemon fused olive oil, divided

⅓ cup honey

¼ cup granulated sugar

¼ cup water

½ tsp ground cinnamon

¼ tsp freshly grated or ground nutmeg

¼ tsp ground cardamom

¼ tsp sea salt

2 cups chopped walnuts

1 egg plus 2 Tbsp Lemon fused olive oil for egg wash

If fiddling with puff pastry is still too much work, you might be interested to hear that I've also used this filling in standard tart shells (using 1 dozen of them). It's simple, delicious, and always a hit! (Cooking temperature and timings remain the same.)

EKMEK

Traditionally, this dessert uses dough from shredded phyllo pastry, but that's very hard to find in North America and it's also very challenging to work with, so I've used lady fingers here instead. Lady fingers hold their texture very well when soaked in syrup, staying crisp on the outside and soft and fluffy on the inside. The Apricot white balsamic vinegar makes this dessert fresh and fruity, and not sickly sweet. Top it with chopped nuts, macerated stone fruit or berries, a drizzle of chocolate, or even a splash of reduced balsamic vinegar to give it the perfect finish.

Grease a 9- × 9-inch baking dish with extra virgin olive oil and arrange the lady fingers in one even layer.

In a small saucepan over medium heat, bring the sugar, water, balsamic, cinnamon stick, and lemon peel to a boil. Turn down the heat and allow it to simmer, uncovered, for about 10 minutes, until a golden, slightly thick syrup forms.

Remove the cinnamon stick and lemon peel. Gently pour the syrup over the lady fingers, making sure they're evenly coated. Place the baking dish in the fridge, uncovered, for at least 15 minutes and up to overnight, to cool completely. This will allow the lady fingers to absorb the syrup and soften.

While the base is cooling, prepare the pastry cream. In a heavy-bottomed saucepan over medium heat, bring the milk to a simmer and then remove from the heat so it doesn't scald or form a skin.

In a mixing bowl, whisk together the sugar, salt, and egg yolks until they're fluffy and a light creamy color. Whisk in the cornstarch. Slowly ladle in some of the warm milk to temper the yolks, then add the yolk-milk mixture back into the simmering milk. Whisking constantly, continue

SERVES
SIX

Base
16 lady fingers

½ cup granulated sugar

¼ cup water

¼ cup Apricot white balsamic vinegar

1 cinnamon stick

Peel from 1 lemon (as intact as possible)

Pastry Cream
2½ cups whole milk

½ cup granulated sugar

¼ tsp sea salt

5 egg yolks

⅓ cup cornstarch

3 Tbsp Lemon fused olive oil

Cream Topping
1 cup heavy (35%) cream

2 Tbsp icing sugar

to heat the custard mixture until it just begins to boil. Boil gently for 30 seconds, then remove from the heat and whisk in the olive oil. Whisk for an additional 30 seconds, then transfer the mixture to a bowl, and cover with plastic wrap, pressing the plastic down onto the custard to prevent a skin from forming. Place the custard in the fridge and allow it to cool completely, 1–2 hours or up to 3 days.

When ready to serve, whisk together the heavy cream and icing sugar to form stiff peaks.

An hour or two before serving, spoon the chilled pastry cream over the chilled lady finger base, smoothing it with a spatula to form an even layer. To serve, slice and top with whipped cream. A spoonful of stewed cherries (page 123) is lovely with this.

This will keep, covered, for up to 3 days in the fridge.

PHYLLO PUMPKIN PIE *with* NUTMEG ICE CREAM

My favorite way to serve this is to place a huge dollop of ice cream right in the center, allowing it to melt and ooze into and between the pieces of phyllo. Although I'm not a fan of phyllo, I find it supereasy to use here as the task is unroll and then roll, and if something happens to break during that rolling process, that is A-OK! It's beautiful, rustic, and delicious, and the ice cream covers any mishaps.

Preheat the oven to 350°F. Line a baking tray with parchment paper.

In a large bowl, mix together the pumpkin purée, cornstarch, egg, and balsamic with the brown sugar and spices until smooth, thick, and creamy. Fold in the walnuts and raisins.

Unroll the thawed phyllo pastry.

Brush the top sheet with some olive oil. Spread ¼ cup of the filling in a long thin line, to within 1 inch of the edge, along the phyllo. Gently fold the 1-inch margin of the sheet over the filling, then gently roll the sheet up to form a long tube. Brush the next sheet with some olive oil to prevent it from drying, then transfer the first tube to the prepared baking sheet. Curl up the tube to form a pinwheel type shape. Don't panic if it breaks—just curl it as tightly as you can, twisting and tucking the ends under to prevent it from uncurling. Place ¼ cup of filling on the next sheet and roll exactly as you did before, but this time, when you're placing it on the baking sheet, wrap it around the first pinwheel, making a larger circle. Repeat with the remaining phyllo and filling until you have a 14-to-16-inch-diameter concentric circle made up of these pumpkin-filled phyllo tubes.

SERVES
SIX

2 cups pumpkin purée
(not pumpkin pie filling;
see sidebar on page 53)

½ cup cornstarch

1 egg

2 Tbsp Apricot white
balsamic vinegar

1 cup brown sugar, packed

1 Tbsp ground cinnamon

1 tsp freshly grated or
ground nutmeg

½ tsp ground allspice

¼ tsp ground cloves

½ cup chopped walnuts

½ cup roughly chopped
golden raisins

1 (8 oz) package phyllo pastry
(20-25 sheets), thawed

½ cup Lemon fused olive oil

1-2 Tbsp granulated sugar

Brush the top of the circle with olive oil and dust with the granulated sugar.

Bake for 35–40 minutes, until golden and crisp. Allow to cool, then transfer to a serving platter or slice directly on the baking tray. Serve with a dollop of nutmeg-scented ice cream in the center or on the side. Dust with icing sugar, if desired.

This is best eaten the day you make it.

NUTMEG ICE CREAM

In a medium-size bowl, whisk together the yolks and sugar until light and frothy. Set aside.

In a large saucepan over medium-low heat (165–170°F), heat the milk, cream, and nutmeg just to a simmer. Do not allow it to come to a boil. Keep it at a simmer while you temper the yolks.

Ladle 1 cup of the warm milk into the yolks, whisking as you do so to temper them. Once the yolks are warm, whisk them into the saucepan with the rest of the milk and continue to simmer until the mixture easily coats the back of a spoon (165°F–170°F). Remove from the heat and pour the mixture through a strainer set over a bowl. Place the bowl in the fridge, uncovered, and allow the ice cream base to cool completely, 4–6 hours.

Meanwhile, prepare your ice cream maker according to the manufacturer's directions.

Pour the cold ice cream base into the ice cream maker and churn according to the manufacturer's instructions. Transfer to a tub or 9- x 5-inch loaf pan and freeze, uncovered, for an additional 6–8 hours, until completely frozen.

This will keep in the freezer, tightly covered, for up to 6 months.

Makes 1 (9- × 5-inch) pan
6 egg yolks
1 cup granulated sugar
1½ cups whole milk
¾ cup heavy (35%) cream
1½ tsp freshly grated
or ground nutmeg

HONEY PIE

This pie is probably better described as a Greek-style cheesecake. It's sweetened with honey and Apricot white balsamic vinegar, so it's not overly sweet, and it has a slightly coarser texture than New York–style cheesecake thanks to the yogurt and ricotta, which also help it hold its shape. This is definitely worth a try!

———————

Preheat the oven to 350°F. Grease an 8-inch springform pan with extra virgin olive oil.

In a large bowl, whisk together the ricotta, yogurt, honey, eggs, and salt until smooth and creamy.

In a small bowl, whisk together 2 Tbsp of the balsamic and the cornstarch to form a creamy, lump-free paste. Drizzle the paste into the ricotta-yogurt mixture and mix well to combine.

Pour the batter into the prepared pan and bake for 35–40 minutes, until the top is golden and a toothpick inserted in the center comes out with only a few wet crumbs. The center should be set and shouldn't jiggle when the cheesecake is moved.

Remove the cake from the oven, run a knife around the outside of the cake, and allow to sit for at least 10 minutes before removing the ring from around the outside of the pan. Let cool completely before serving.

Meanwhile, in a small saucepan over medium heat, bring the remaining ¼ cup of balsamic to a gentle boil. Swirling the pan to keep the vinegar moving, cook it down for 2–3 minutes, until slightly golden. Gently pour this warm reduction over the cake slices immediately before serving, or drizzle it onto serving plates before placing the slices on top. The vinegar reduction will cool when it touches the cake and create a caramel effect.

SERVES
SIX

2 cups ricotta cheese

1 cup plain Greek yogurt
(store-bought or homemade,
see page 17)

½ cup honey

3 eggs

½ tsp sea salt

¼ cup + 2 Tbsp Apricot white
.balsamic vinegar

1 Tbsp cornstarch

LEMON YOGURT SOUFFLÉ

Light and fluffy with a rich custard base, this soufflé is an easy way to use up extra eggs that are crowding your fridge. The flavor is very mild, which makes this dessert superversatile. Serve on its own to fully enjoy the subtle creamy lemony flavor, or serve with stewed cherries (page 123) to brighten the flavors and add even more character.

————————————

Preheat the oven to 350°F. Drizzle some of the olive oil into eight 6 oz ramekins or a deep 8-inch round baking dish. Spread it evenly around the dish, using your fingers or a paper towel. Sprinkle the dish immediately with sugar and shake to ensure all the edges are coated. Set aside.

Separate the eggs into two bowls. Beat the whites to stiff peaks and set aside.

Whisk the egg yolks with the 2 Tbsp olive oil and sugar to form a creamy, pale yellow mixture. Gently whisk in the cornstarch, ensuring it's evenly distributed and the mixture is still smooth. Whisk in the yogurt until the mixture is as smooth as possible. A few lumps are OK. Fold in the whipped egg whites using a rubber or silicone spatula.

Prepare a water bath in a large baking dish. Arrange the ramekins so they all fit snugly. Fill the baking dish with warm water.

Carefully spoon the soufflé mix into the ramekins until they are three-quarters full.

Bake for 20 minutes for ramekins, 25–30 for one large dish, or until the top is puffed and golden brown. Remove from the oven and let sit for 5 minutes to rest. Dust with icing sugar and serve.

These are best enjoyed the day you make them.

SERVES
EIGHT
————

2 Tbsp Lemon fused olive oil, plus extra to grease the dishes

1 cup granulated sugar, plus extra for dusting the dishes

5 eggs

¼ cup cornstarch

1½ cups plain Greek yogurt (store-bought or homemade, see page 17)

Icing sugar for garnish

LOUKOUMADES (DONUTS with HONEY and WALNUTS)

These are basically a Greek version of a doughnut hole—jazzed up with lots of honey and nuts in ultimate Greek style, of course. The Lemon fused olive oil helps keep the donuts extra moist and rich, so when you bite in, it's all fluffy, sticky goodness!

Preheat the oven to 250°F. When it comes to temperature, turn it off.

In the bowl of a stand mixer fitted with the whisk attachment, whisk together the flour, sugar, yeast, and baking powder.

In a heavy-bottomed saucepan over medium heat, heat the water, milk, and olive oil to 110°F.

With the mixer running on low speed, slowly pour in the liquid, allowing it to fully incorporate with the flour mixture. Increase the speed slightly and continue to whisk for 3–4 more minutes, ensuring the dough is fully combined. It will be very sticky. Remove the bowl from the mixer, cover with a dry tea towel, and place it in the warmed oven for 30 minutes to rise. It will puff up and be bubbly.

For the syrup, in a small saucepan over medium-low heat, whisk together the honey, lemon juice, cinnamon, and salt and allow to simmer gently for 1–2 minutes. Turn the heat to low to keep the syrup warm.

Place paper towels under a wire rack.

When the dough has risen, place 2–3 inches of oil in a heavy-bottomed saucepan, ensuring it's deep enough to submerge the loukoumades. Heat the oil to 350°F. Using a spoon, or a small ice cream scoop, dipped in olive oil, gently scoop 1 Tbsp of batter into the warm oil. Allow the dough to drop into the pot. Repeat until

Makes about
2 dozen loukoumades

Donuts

2 cups all-purpose flour

2 Tbsp granulated sugar

2 tsp quick-rising yeast

1 tsp baking powder

¾ cup water

¾ cup whole milk

2 Tbsp Lemon fused olive oil

3-4 cups mild-flavored oil for deep-frying

¼ cup chopped walnuts

Honey Syrup

¾ cup honey

2 Tbsp lemon juice

¼ tsp ground cinnamon

¼ tsp sea salt

there are several donuts in the oil, being careful not to overcrowd the pan. I usually make four to six at a time. Fry for 2 minutes, then using a slotted spoon, turn the donuts over and fry for 45 seconds to 1 minute to cook them evenly on both sides. When the donuts are golden, remove them from the oil using the slotted spoon and set them on the prepared wire rack to drain off any excess oil. Allow the oil to come back up to temperature and repeat with the remaining dough.

When all the donuts have been fried, pile them up on a serving platter, drizzle with the warm syrup, and sprinkle with walnuts. Alternatively, in a large bowl, place half the donuts, drizzle them with half the syrup, and toss to coat evenly. Arrange them on a serving platter and sprinkle with half the walnuts. Repeat with the remaining donuts, syrup, and walnuts, piling them all on top of the first batch.

These are best served immediately and enjoyed the day you make them, but they'll keep in an airtight container for up to 3 days at room temperature.

CHRISTMAS COOKIES

During the holidays, two kinds of cookies are a staple in every Greek home—these, and a golden cookie drenched in honey and topped with walnuts. These have a unique texture, as they're toasty, almost biscuit-like on the outside, and soft on the inside. The Lemon fused olive oil ensures that they stay moist and adds a lovely lemon note to the batter.

Preheat the oven to 325°F. Line a baking tray with parchment paper.

In the bowl of a stand mixer fitted with the whisk attachment, or using hand beaters, whip the butter and olive oil together for at least 5–7 minutes, until very light and fluffy and fully incorporated. Continue to beat as you add the yolks, one at a time and fully incorporating each one, and then, still beating, slowly add ½ cup of the icing sugar and the baking powder. Beat for another 5 minutes. Pour in the balsamic and then slowly sift in the flour. Using a wooden spoon, mix to form a soft dough.

Spoon 1 Tbsp of the dough into your hand and roll into a ball, then place on the prepared baking tray about 1 inch apart. Place tray in the fridge and allow the cookies to cool for 1 hour. Remove from the fridge and bake for 7 minutes, then turn down the oven to 250°F without opening the oven door and bake for an additional 5 minutes. (You don't need to wait until the oven reaches temperature to start timing this.)

Remove from the heat and allow to cool on a wire rack. The cookies will be light in color, but slightly golden on the bottom. Repeat with the remaining dough.

Dust ¾ cup of icing sugar onto a serving plate, pile the cookies on top, and then dust with the remaining icing sugar—the more the better!

Makes 2 dozen cookies

½ cup unsalted butter at room temperature

⅓ cup Lemon fused olive oil

2 egg yolks

2 cups icing sugar, divided

½ tsp baking powder

1 tsp Apricot white balsamic vinegar

1 cup cake-and-pastry flour

The butter in this recipe is essential. Mixing it with the olive oil keeps the cookies from spreading too much during baking and adds that signature shortbread richness. The reality is even I can't make a shortbread cookie without at least a little bit of butter.

GREEK NEW YEAR'S CAKE

Delicious at any time of year, this pound-style cake is traditionally made for New Year's Eve and is cut at midnight. Thanks to the Lemon fused olive oil, the cake is flavorful yet subtle, fluffy in texture, and has a lovely moist crumb. Dust it with icing sugar or drizzle it with an Apricot white balsamic vinegar icing sugar glaze (shown here).

———

Preheat the oven to 350°F. Drizzle a 9-inch round cake pan with some of the olive oil. Rub it in well to ensure all the surfaces are greased, then dust with some flour, and shake to ensure the pan is evenly coated in flour and any excess has been discarded.

In a large bowl, whisk together the flour, baking powder, baking soda, and salt.

In a separate bowl, whisk together the sugar and olive oil until fluffy and creamy. Add the eggs, one at a time, whisking well to incorporate each addition. Whisk in the yogurt, then one-third of the flour mixture, then half the milk, the second third of the flour mixture, then the remaining milk and then flour to create a completely smooth batter.

Pour the batter into the prepared pan and bake for 45–50 minutes, until the top is golden brown and a toothpick inserted into the center comes out with only a few moist crumbs attached.

Remove the cake from the oven and run a knife around the outside. Let it sit for 10–15 minutes, then gently remove it from the pan and allow to completely cool on a wire rack.

For the glaze, in a small saucepan over low heat, warm the balsamic. Remove from the heat and begin to whisk in the icing sugar. When fully combined and lump-free, drizzle over the surface of the cake. Sprinkle the lemon zest over the top, and allow to cool and dry completely before serving.

SERVES

SIX-EIGHT

Makes 1 (9-inch) cake

Cake

2½ cups cake-and-pastry flour

2 tsp baking powder

½ tsp baking soda

½ tsp sea salt

1 cup granulated sugar

½ cup Lemon fused olive oil

4 eggs

½ cup plain Greek yogurt
(store-bought or homemade,
see page 17)

¾ cup 2% milk

To finish

¼ cup Apricot white
balsamic vinegar

2 cups icing sugar

1 tsp grated lemon zest

MENUS

EVERYDAY FAVORITES

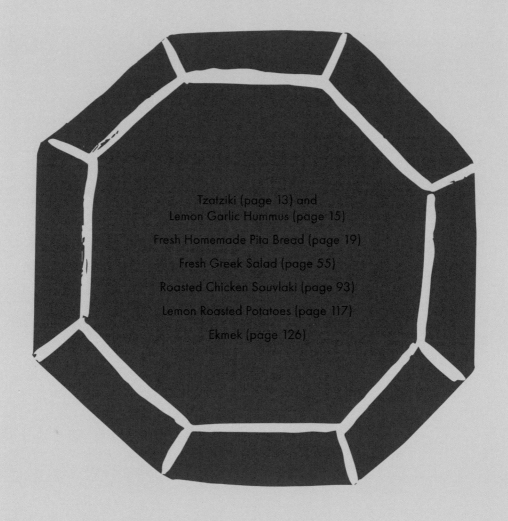

SPECIAL
OCCASION FEAST

Spanakopita Puffs (page 35)

Lemon Rice Soup (page 44)

Fresh Leek and Olive Salad (page 57)

Roasted Leg of Lamb (page 75)

Seafood Pilaf (page 103)

Greek New Year's Cake (page 145)

SUMMER COOKOUT

Baked Feta (page 25)

Tomato and Kalamata Flatbread (page 23)

Lemon Dill and Black-Eyed Pea Salad (page 61)

Greek-Style Pork Ribs (page 87)

Lamb Sliders with Pickled Onion Slaw (page 71)

Baklava Turnovers (page 125)

COZY WINTER COMFORT

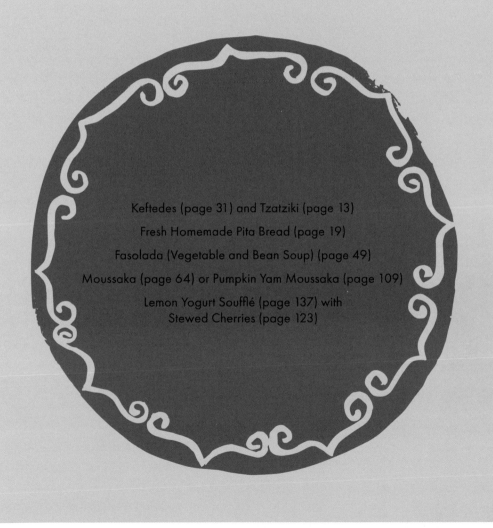

Keftedes (page 31) and Tzatziki (page 13)

Fresh Homemade Pita Bread (page 19)

Fasolada (Vegetable and Bean Soup) (page 49)

Moussaka (page 64) or Pumpkin Yam Moussaka (page 109)

Lemon Yogurt Soufflé (page 137) with
Stewed Cherries (page 123)

METRIC CONVERSIONS CHART

VOLUME	
⅛ tsp	0.5 mL
¼ tsp	1 mL
½ tsp	2.5 mL
¾ tsp	4 mL
1 tsp	5 mL
1½ tsp	7.5 mL
2 tsp	10 mL
1 Tbsp	15 mL
4 tsp	20 mL
2 Tbsp	30 mL
3 Tbsp	45 mL
¼ cup/4 Tbsp	60 mL
5 Tbsp	75 mL
⅓ cup	80 mL
½ cup	125 mL
⅔ cup	160 mL
¾ cup	185 mL
1 cup	250 mL

VOLUME	
1¼ cups	310 mL
1½ cups	375 mL
1¾ cups	435 mL
2 cups/1 pint	500 mL
2¼ cups	560 mL
2½ cups	625 mL
3 cups	750 mL
3½ cups	875 mL
4 cups/1 quart	1 L
4½ cups	1.125 L
5 cups	1.25 L
5½ cups	1.375 L
6 cups	1.5 L
6½ cups	1.625 L
7 cups	1.75 L
8 cups	2 L
12 cups	3 L

VOLUME	
¼ fl oz	7.5 mL
½ fl oz	15 mL
¾ fl oz	22 mL
1 fl oz	30 mL
1½ fl oz	45 mL
2 fl oz	60 mL
3 fl oz	90 mL
4 fl oz	125 mL
5 fl oz	160 mL
6 fl oz	185 mL
8 fl oz	250 mL
24 fl oz	750 mL

WEIGHT	
1 oz	30 g
2 oz	60 g
3 oz	90 g
¼ lb/4 oz	125 g
5 oz	150 g
6 oz	175 g
½ lb/8 oz	250 g
9 oz	270 g
10 oz	300 g
¾ lb/12 oz	375 g
14 oz	400 g
1 lb	500 g
1½ lb	750 g
2 lb	1 kg
2½ lb	1.25 kg
3 lb	1.5 kg
4 lb	1.8 kg
5 lb	2.3 kg
5½ lb	2.5 kg
6 lb	2.7 kg

LENGTH	
⅛ inch	3 mm
¼ inch	6 mm
⅜ inch	9 mm
½ inch	1.25 cm
¾ inch	2 cm
1 inch	2.5 cm
1½ inches	4 cm
2 inches	5 cm
3 inches	8 cm
4 inches	10 cm
4½ inches	11 cm
5 inches	12 cm
6 inches	15 cm
7 inches	18 cm
8 inches	20 cm
8½ inches	22 cm
9 inches	23 cm
10 inches	25 cm
11 inches	28 cm
12 inches	30 cm

OVEN TEMPERATURE	
40°F	5°C
120°F	49°C
125°F	51°C
130°F	54°C
135°F	57°C
140°F	60°C
145°F	63°C
150°F	66°C
155°F	68°C
160°F	71°C
165°F	74°C
170°F	77°C
180°F	82°C
200°F	95°C
225°F	107°C
250°F	120°C
275°F	140°C
300°F	150°C
325°F	160°C
350°F	180°C
375°F	190°C
400°F	200°C
425°F	220°C
450°F	230°C
475°F	240°C
500°F	260°C

CAN SIZES	
4 oz	114 mL
14 oz	398 mL
19 oz	540 mL
28 oz	796 mL

ACKNOWLEDGMENTS

Thank you to the friends, loved ones, and faithful customers who have inspired these recipes and encouraged me on this journey. As my food-nerdiness evolves and my love for olive oil and vinegar deepens, I continue to be amazed at all the wonderful people in my life who lift me up and bring it all together.

Steve, here we go again with a million dirty dishes invading our kitchen! Between the whirlwind of recipe testing, photo shoots, and the legs of lamb landing in the oven at 4am, people piling into our small apartment to eat all the leftovers, late-night grocery runs, and ensuring that Cedrik doesn't feel unloved; words cannot fully express my gratitude for you. You put all the pieces together and you make this dream a reality. Thank you for supporting my vision and walking beside me every step of the way.

Danielle, you are the best partner in crime, and these recipes would be nothing without your exceptional talent for making images come alive and jump off the page. Working with you is my favorite, not to mention how much I love the chance to cook for your family, enjoy our late night talks and cider, and treasure the cozy nights in your beautiful cottage. I look forward to our days together and can't wait to see what comes next!

Taryn, thank you for catching our dreams, for falling in love with olive oil and vinegar, and for making the book so beautiful and vivid. If it wasn't for you and your vision, none of this would be happening. You are a rock, and you and the TouchWood team work tirelessly to bring the dream to life.

This book also wouldn't be possible without the Olive the Senses team. You are so capable and patient, and have held down the fort right from the beginning. Thank you for letting me take time to make this book happen, and for loving our customers, sharing my inspiration and passion, and running with all of it. I have learned so much from you. What we create together is the best, and none of this would be possible without you, your taste buds, fridge space, and endless energy. From the late-night cooking adventures to morning check-ins that include three versions of homemade yogurt-turned-into-tzatziki, I thank you from the bottom of my heart.

INDEX

EMILY LYCOPOLUS is a recipe developer, the author of six olive oil-focused cookbooks, and a level two olive oil sommelier. She is the co-founder of eatcreative.ca, a food-driven creative content agency, and she also reviews olive oils and shares educational articles as The Olive Oil Critic at oliveoilcritic.com. Her family owns an olive grove in central Italy, where her love of olive oil began.

DANIELLE (DL) ACKEN is a Canadian-born international food photographer who splits her time between London, UK and her farm studio on Canada's beautiful Salt Spring Island. A self-proclaimed compulsive traveler, her photography is inspired by the multitude of palettes and moods found throughout her wanderings. See her work at dlacken.com.

Edited by Lesley Cameron
Designed and illustrated by Tree Abraham

LIBRARY AND ARCHIVES CANADA CATALOGUING IN PUBL
Lycopolus, Emily, 1985-, author
Greece : recipes for olive oil and vinegar lovers /
Emily Lycopolus; photographs by D.L. Acken.
Includes index.

Issued in print and electronic formats.
ISBN 978-1-77151-234-3 (hardcover)

1. Cooking (Olive oil). 2. Cooking (Vinegar). 3. Olive oil. 4. Vi
5. Cooking, Greek. 6. Cookbooks. I. Title.

TX819.042L924 2017   641.6'463   C201790

We acknowledge the financial support of the Government of Canada throu
Fund and the province of British Columbia through the Book Publish

TouchWood Editions acknowledges that the land on which we live and v
traditional territories of the Lkwungen (Esquimalt and Songhees), Malahat,
T'Sou-ke and W̱-SÁNEĆ (Pauquachin, Tsartlip, Tsawout, Tseycum

This book was produced using FSC®-certified, acid-free pa
processed chlorine free, and printed with soya-based ink

PRINTED IN CHINA

27 26 25 24 23   4 5